Heritage, Communit

DUCKWORTH DEBATES IN ARCHAEOLOGY

Series editor: Richard Hodges

Heritage, Communities and Archaeology

Laurajane Smith &
Emma Waterton

Duckworth

First published in 2009 by
Gerald Duckworth & Co. Ltd.
90-93 Cowcross Street
London EC1M 6BF
Tel: 020 7490 7300
Fax: 020 7490 0080
info@duckworth-publishers.co.uk
www.ducknet.co.uk

A catalogue record for this book is available
from the British Library

ISBN 978 0 7156 3681 7

Typeset by Ray Davies
Printed and bound in Great Britain by
CPI Antony Rowe, Chippenham, Wiltshire

Contents

Figures

Abbreviations

AHD	Authorised Heritage Discourse
AHM	Archaeological Heritage Management
BAJR	British Archaeological Jobs Resource
BBC	British Broadcasting Corporation
BBS	Bulletin Board System
CARP	Community Archaeology Research Project, Lincoln
CAPQ	Community Archaeology Project at Quseir, Egypt
CBA	Council for British Archaeology
CCGG	Cawood Castle Garth Group
CHM	Cultural Heritage Management
CHT	Castleford Heritage Trust
CMC	Computer-Mediated Communication
COBG	Consortium of Black Groups
CRM	Cultural Resource Management
DCMS	Department for Culture, Media and Sport
HER	Historic Environment Record
HPR	Heritage Protection Review
ICOMOS	International Council on Monuments and Sites
IM	Instant Messaging
LDF	Local Development Framework
MLA	Museums, Libraries and Archives Council
MUD	Multiple User Domain
NAPincl	National Action Plans for Social Inclusion

Abbreviations

NGO	Non-Governmental Organisation
NDPB	Non-Departmental Public Body
PPG	Planning Policy Guidance
SCI	Statement of Community Involvement
SMR	Sites and Monuments Record
UNESCO	United Nations Educational, Scientific and Cultural Organisation
WHC	World Heritage Convention

Acknowledgements

We would like to thank Deborah Blake, Editorial Director at Duckworth, for her patience, and acknowledge and thank those individuals and organisations that accommodated our requests for their time and input: Dr Daniel Hull, Council for British Archaeology, Dr Jon Kenny, York Archaeological Trust, and Dr Keith Emerick, English Heritage (York) – although we acknowledge that the opinions we have expressed within are our own.

We are especially grateful to the many people from the Castleford Heritage Trust and the Cawood Castle Garth Group who generously offered us their time, patience and knowledge. In particular, we are indebted to Carole Birtwhistle, Margaret Brearley, Alison Drake, Ian Dersley, Jane Dersley, Lorna Malkin and Margaret Squires, all of whom extended extraordinary levels of kindness, enthusiasm and support.

As always, we would like to thank Gary Campbell for his intellectual stimulation, impeccable editorial skills and encouragement. Thanks also to Dr Steve Watson for his support and humour, and Alison Drake for her inspiration.

Finally, we acknowledge financial assistance from the British Academy Small Grants scheme for funding work undertaken by Laurajane in Castleford, and the Engineering and Physical Sciences Research Council (EPSRC, on behalf of RCUK, fellowship reference number EP/E500579/1) for Emma.

Introduction

This book is aimed at making people think about 'community', heritage and archaeology. It is in part polemical, and as such we are not interested in making people feel comfortable about 'community', which, to be blunt, has been drawn on for comfort for too long, 'like a roof under which we shelter in heavy rain, like a fireplace at which we warm our hands on a frosty day' (Bauman 2001: 1). At the same time as we work to take people out of their comfort zones, we also want to stress the massive potential that working with 'communities' has for the heritage sector. However, before we discuss that, we need to clarify the concepts of 'community' and 'heritage', and address some core issues relevant to the three main interest groups for whom this book is written.

For professional workers in the heritage sector – archaeologists, museum workers, architects, art historians, public historians, etc. – we have a very direct message. You are a community, but just one community of interest among many others. Once we cut through the rhetoric of custodianship and stewardship, and the authority accorded to expert knowledge by society in general and government and state bodies in particular, experts in the heritage sector are just another community with an interest in the past. The difference is that they get paid for it, and define themselves and their careers by their engagement with the past, but their interest in the past is no more or less legitimate, or worthy of respect, than anyone else's.

For decision-makers in government, and those who frame and deliver policy, the yoking together of 'community' and 'heritage' has been far less effective than they might have hoped. This is largely because of the ill-defined assumptions policymakers have made about communities, heritage and social inclusion. While staying out of the rain and warming their hands at the fire of 'community', policymakers have lost sight of the fact that ticking a few boxes about including working-class and ethnic minorities in visitor targets has confused more effective marketing with democratically extending the idea of what heritage is, and how it should be promoted. Rather than asking why the 'socially excluded' should visit stately homes and art galleries, perhaps the question should be asked why the middle-classes aren't visiting, for example, the many local museums that commemorate working-class life in industrial regions, or museums and heritage centres that address less comforting aspects of history, such as slavery, the experiences of migrant communities and colonialism. Assuming that 'social inclusion' means one community visiting the heritage of another, but not the other way around, is simply cultural assimilation, and makes many unwarranted assumptions about who should visit what, and why.

For those active in communities there are also some challenges in this book. For many people, 'community' and 'heritage' are comfortably self-evident, defined by place and shared histories, and often ethnicity and nationality, and redolent of shared values and their celebration. However, communities take many forms, are often riven by dissent, and bear the burden of uncomfortable histories. They are often defined by the articulate and the privileged, who are readily recognised by policymakers and professionals, leaving others to some peripheral status. Diversity and social difference, both between and within communities, must be recognised not just by policymakers and professionals, but also by communities themselves. This book therefore starts from these critical observations about 'community' and 'heritage', and we suggest that heritage experts, policymakers and community activists need to engage in debate lest the use of the terms 'community' and 'heritage' remain warm, cuddly and lacking in substance.

The power the term 'community' has should not be understated: about a decade ago, Barrie Sharpe (1998: 39) published an article in the field of natural resource management in Cameroon in which he quoted the Director of the South Bakundu Forest Regeneration Project's remark that 'if they don't have a community we'll make them form one, and then we'll order them to participate'. Admittedly, this was uttered in a context rife with corruption, where limits were imposed on freedom of expression, and thus may seem a somewhat disingenuous statement with which to open a volume dealing with heritage and archaeology in the predominantly Western world. However, it does reveal the powerful and evidently far-reaching influence of the notion of 'community'. What we draw from it is the degree to which 'community' has become near-mandatory, an almost daily construction, or something that borders on a pathological compulsion, extending beyond the limits of our own disciplines and cultural specificities. This escalation of interest can be seen from the spate of voluntary organisations, local governance initiatives and grassroots projects using the prefix 'community', to the large funding bodies, national policy initiatives and international economic aid directives, all using the term with impunity (Kumar 2005). Certainly, it has attractiveness in a policy sense, but what exactly drives this obsession with the idea of 'community'?

The rhetoric of 'community' is used to make ourselves *feel good* about the work we do as heritage professionals, particularly as we become increasingly aware of the politically difficult nature of our work – it becomes *the right thing to do*. It is a term that is 'never used in a negative sense', nor, for that matter, do people ever 'say that they are against "community"' (Kumar 2005: 277). It is for this reason that the concept turns up with such frequency within the heritage sector (Arantes 2007). This development of a community rhetoric, as Cooper (2008: 26) notes, has become one of the most enduring characteristics of present-day heritage management and archaeological practice, *despite* the fact that we do not yet have a clear understanding of its varied uses and implications.

If the idea of 'community' most frequently embraced is something that is 'good', 'safe' and 'comfortable', it is with an acute sense of paradox that we note its emergence out of a distinctly *un*comfortable and challenging context. Indeed, perhaps the most powerful impetus behind our talk of 'community' is agitation by Indigenous people in colonial settler societies to have their voices, and views of the past, heard. In this context, much of what has been described as 'community archaeology' emerged as a consequence of sustained challenges to the imposition of authorised accounts and understandings of heritage and archaeology onto Indigenous peoples. Similarly, tensions emerging out of the perceived fragility of the experiences and knowledges of the so-called Third World also triggered an interest in community mobilisation as a means of using local resources to address 'local' problems (Hudson 2004: 252). Hot on the heels of this recognition of a community impetus in post-colonial and Third World contexts was the realisation that some of the lessons we have learnt might have broader relevance in discrete cases within the West. This, for us, seems a confusing situation. If politically fraught, complex and haunting issues succeeded in raising our awareness of community interests in the first place, why, then, do we deal with these issues within archaeology and heritage management on an episodic (Zielinski 2007) or case-by-case basis, leaving our overarching understanding of 'community' as something that is unusually and unambiguously 'good'?

To answer this question, it is necessary to revisit the relationships between heritage, archaeology and community, not only in terms of their historical association, but by unpacking the prevalent images of 'community' in heritage studies and critically examining implementations of community work around the world. At the same time, we argue for a reconsideration of the implications of this dominant approach to community archaeology and heritage, particularly in terms of how archaeological knowledge and heritage expertise are *used* in these situations, and the wider consequences our practices have for a range of social problems. Of course, this inevitably draws the heritage profession beyond the parameters of archaeological sites or episodes of engaging with a museum, local landscape or collective memories. Indeed, it requires the profession to think more clearly and responsibly about what else is happening – or what else is at stake – within the management process, forcing us to grapple with the unwieldy areas of social justice (see Chapter 4). This will at times be painful, especially when we are asked to acknowledge the less positive aspects of our work and the uses it is put to, not least when it is harnessed to wider public policies that skate closer to messages of racism and cultural assimilation than they do to social inclusion (see Chapters 3 and 5). Yet the relationship between heritage professionals and communities need not be negative; indeed there are many positive case studies documenting useful community engagement in the literature. However, one of the central arguments of this volume is that it is the *process* by which community groups are engaged with that is important, and this should be a process that is open to – and accepting of – difference in the richest sense of the term. This orientation to difference allows for an awareness of competing definitions and understandings of the same thing, prompting useful and rewarding two-way exchanges of ideas, experiences and interpretations of heritage. It is only in this way that we can begin to acknowledge the systemic and theoretical blinkers that prevent us from engaging with community groups holistically and honestly. Indeed, it is only from such a position that we can convincingly argue that the idea of 'community' should be a central concern for *all* archaeological and heritage practice.

What do we mean by 'community'?

Before developing our argument, there are three definitions that we need to pin down. Foremost, what do we mean by 'community' in relation to archaeology and heritage? Our reading of the related literature has revealed a bewildering array of terms used in the description and implementation of community projects. These include: community archaeology, community-engaged, community-based, community-led, outreach, public archaeology, Indigenous archaeology, community collaboration, community facilitation, postcolonial archaeology, public education, democratic archaeology, community heritage, participatory archaeology and alternative archaeology. Of these, it is perhaps 'public archaeology' that has become the most visible, originally coined by Charles McGimsey in 1972 and now the title of an international journal. Community engagement can also be undertaken for a wide-range of reasons. Consultation with community groups may occur as part of archaeological/heritage management work, as part of educational outreach programmes, or from a desire to make research work 'relevant' to communities. Community volunteers may participate in excavation and other projects, and communities themselves may approach experts for support, help or guidance in archaeological or heritage projects that they have initiated.

Although a variety of phrases and aims exist, it is the phrases 'community collaboration' and 'community-based' that are the more promising, both in terms of describing the range of aims for community engagement and in allowing the most room for the development of effective engagements. Two of the most widely – and positively – cited approaches to 'community' are Moser et al.'s discussion of the Community Archaeology Project at Quseir (CAPQ), Egypt, and Greer et al.'s exploration of experiences of community-based archaeology in Australia. Tully (2007: 157) notes that the CAPQ project was the 'first academic grant awarded to a community archaeology project' and has become something of a quintessential example. Perhaps best received is the set of methodological components considered essential for conducting community projects:

1. communication and collaboration;
2. employment and training;
3. public presentation;
4. interviews and oral history;
5. educational resources;
6. photographic and video archive;
7. community-controlled merchandising (Moser et al. 2002: 229).

Collectively, these steps aim to cover archaeological projects from beginning to end, and are based on the proposition that 'at every step in the project at least partial control remains with the community' (Marshall 2002: 211). They are underpinned by a belief in the need for a collaborative and transformative practice that extends beyond the standard question of ethics, and are based upon the inevitability of conflicts, tensions and dissent (Moser et al. 2002: 243). Of the seven components listed above, only two – communication/collaboration and interviews/oral history – have reached a high level of representation across more recent projects (Tully 2007). The seven components provide a baseline of practical points for undertaking collaborative work, although there are two key limitations. First, they infer a case-by-case methodology that need be applied only in certain circumstances, or in those projects that self-consciously set out to be about the community. Second, while the sharing of information within the components is laudable, it continues to reinforce a somewhat unidirectional flow of knowledge, as witnessed by the tendency to *invite* community members into the process. However, the CAPQ was set up some ten years ago. Our aim is not to test or adhere to the continued validity of this methodological baseline, but to provoke debate *beyond* these seven principles.

The haunting colonial context of Australian archaeology has facilitated an articulated debate about community interest and as such, the second approach we draw attention to emerges out of work by Shelley Greer and her notion of 'community-based' research. This is defined as 'empowering communities by contributing to the construction of local identity' using an inter*active* orientation to communication (Greer et al. 2002: 268; Clarke 2002). This approach explicitly emerges out of a dialogue between archaeologists and Indigenous people and is an attempt to incorporate the challenges and dissatisfaction of Indigenous people into the discipline of archaeology, and destabilise the assumed prominence of archaeological knowledge above all other ways of seeing/knowing the past. It is thus built upon an awareness of the political nature of heritage, and the capacity for heritage to be used as 'lodestones for group memory and identity' in the present (Greer et al. 2002: 282). It is, to borrow from Clarke (2002), a re/negotiated experience. In relation to the very notion of 'community', Greer et al. (2002) make mention of several key points. They, like Swadlhin Sen (2002), caution against assumptions that a community is a homogeneous unit; instead it is a heterogeneous and changing aggregate of people. As well, membership of a community should not necessarily be defined by – or tied to – a person's geographical residency. A significant assumption often made is that community *is* 'local' – that it is geographically-based. While there are communities that define themselves geographically, communities may be defined and linked by a range of social and cultural experiences, and/or political experiences and aspirations that transcend geography and are, in fact, geographically widespread. For instance, shared experiences influenced by ethnicity, class, gender, age, religion, sexual orientation, political beliefs, and so forth, are factors around which communities may define themselves. It is also important to acknowledge that individuals may belong to more than one community at any one time. Moreover, engagements with heritage and the past will not be limited to one key community group, but will inevitably revolve around a convergence of often conflicting interests and aspirations (Marshall 2002: 216).

Another important aspect of communities is the recognition that they may self-define, and engagements with such communities may be difficult. This is complicated as the automatic response of experts is often to try to manage the situation and define how engagement with communities will progress. But we cannot 'make' people conform to our expectations nor 'order them to participate' in ways we control. Engagement is often fraught, and tensions, misunderstandings and confusion between expertise and communities are not confined to interactions within cross-cultural contexts. Moreover, in avoiding these discomforts and difficulties, there is often a tendency to confine our interactions to the well-organised, vocal and geographically 'local' community. However, if we want to engage properly with the idea of 'community', we must address our discomforts.

The second term to clarify is that of power. While the above authors encourage a context within which competing groups cooperate and collaborate, creating such a context is not always that simple. Indeed, it requires an explicit assessment of the sustained failure to acknowledge not only the existence of unequal power relations both within and surrounding heritage and archaeological practice, but also the outcomes of those relations. What does it *do* for, and to, those attempting to engage in collaborative projects, in terms of individuals, groups and societies, and *how* have those power relations come about? This questioning of power will move beyond a simplistic assessment of who prevails in terms of decision-making (Richardson 2007: 30) to examine those practices and assumptions that *limit* public, community and non-expert involvement to a discrete variety of projects or instances within the wider management process. The distribution of resources, both symbolic and material, and the conditions available for parity of participation and issues of control are vital considerations. As are the 'rules of the game' (Richardson 2007: 31), or those facets of power that allow expertise to suppress, thwart or obscure some heritage issues, while drawing others to the foreground.

The third and final definition draws explicitly from the above understanding of 'community' and 'power': archaeologists, heritage managers and museum professionals can be defined as a community group themselves, on a par with other groups encountered in this volume – this 'community of expertise' will be referred to as 'heritage professionals' hereafter. The work of Julie Lahn (1996) and her critique of the disciplinary identity of archaeology draws attention to the degree to which self-image, group-image, status, ownership and control are bound up with the ability of archaeologists to make pronouncements about the past and maintain political and professional control over its material remains. We can see that in some ways things have moved on since Lahn first presented these criticisms, but her prediction that the archaeological community would seek, unconsciously or not, new ways of asserting their authority – and, in effect, prevent the conditions for a genuine politics of recognition – continues to ring true. One source that heritage professionals have turned to in reinventing that identity is the realm of community work. For us this is critical, as it forces us to see ourselves in terms of our own interests, needs, desires and aspirations, and acknowledge that the ways in which we utilise heritage are no different from those of the groups we attempt to represent.

1

Heritage, communities and archaeology: a history

Introduction

Talk of 'community' is endemic in much of the heritage sector in England, resulting in what McClanahan (2007) has labelled 'the cult of community'. For many, this is a consequence of New Labour's and Tony Blair's fixation with John Macmurray's Christian communitarianism (Fairclough 2000; Levitas 2005: 105). With the introduction of policies such as the *New Deal for Communities*, the recent emergence of the governmental department *Communities and Local Government* (formerly the Office of the Deputy Prime Minister), and the setting up of the *Community Cohesion Unit*, it does indeed seem as though 'community' is at the heart of New Labour politics (Blair 2005; see also Blair 2000, 2001). Likewise, the recent introduction of a requirement that all local authorities produce Local Development Frameworks (LDF), including a Statement of Community Involvement (SCI), is also indicative of its significance. Consequently, as a recent volume of *Heritage Counts* identifies, the idea of 'community' has reached 'the forefront of the work in the sector' (English Heritage 2006a: 2).

This increased focus on 'community' is also mirrored popularly, as evidenced by a long-term and wide-scale interest in public history/archaeology in Britain, captured by the 162 heritage-related programmes broadcast on television during 2005-06 (English Heritage 2006a), such as *Time Team* (Channel 4), *Meet the Ancestors* (BBC and UKTV), *Who Do You Think You Are* (BBC) and *Restoration* (BBC). By 2006, English Heritage and the National Trust collectively enjoyed a four-million-strong membership, with 90% of participants in the 2007 DCMS-led *Taking Part Survey* citing the importance of 'heritage' for improving local places (DCMS 2007: 29). Simultaneously, visible institutional kudos have been attached to the term 'community', resulting in the establishment of full-time community heritage/archaeology posts across the UK, the development of the Outreach Department within English Heritage in 2003, and long-running heritage projects such as the Community Landscape Project in Devon (2001-present) and the Community Archaeology Research Project (CARP) in Lincoln (1999-present). Similar projects have also been ongoing in an international context, including Archaeology in Annapolis, USA, since 1981 (Leone et al. 1987), the Levi Jordan Plantation Historical Society, USA, since 1993 (McDavid 2004), and the Community Archaeology Project at Quseir, Egypt (CAPQ), since 1998 (Moser et al. 2002).

Despite the contemporary ubiquity of the term, the aim of this chapter is to suggest that increasing community focus is not of recent provenance: indeed, it has been with us for some time. The chapter argues that a limited position has been crafted for community groups within the management process, one that decisively differs from that afforded to heritage professionals, particularly in terms of their respective abilities to identify and influence heritage values, meanings and experiences. Many of the tensions and conflicts that arise between community groups and heritage professionals revolve around these positions, which are based upon a misunderstanding of the significant stake each group has in the management process.

A fireside at which we warm our hands[1]

The history of community research is characterised by periods of intense study separated by phases of conceptual anxiety and misuse. Across this history, the term 'community' has see-sawed from an association with empirically rich investigations

of social relationships to theoretically weak and nostalgic representations (Hoggett 1997: 5; see also Stacey 1969). It is therefore unsurprising that the term has appeared, disappeared and
reappeared within the sociological and anthropological lexicon
a number of times, making a recent a come-back (Hoggett 1997:
6). The burgeoning literature and simultaneous policy emphasis on the notion of 'community' in the last few years can
therefore best be described as something of a revival of a focus
that initially developed in the 1950s and 1960s, and reappeared in the 1980s and early 1990s (Crow & Allan 1994).
Indeed, within heritage studies community research is now
enjoying its third peak. Thus, while the subject has experienced periods of avoidance and obfuscation within the academy, it remains, as Day and Murdoch (1993: 85) point out, 'a
term that just will not lie down'.

While there is no clear and specific history for the development of community research in heritage studies, we will
focus upon three distinct phases: the 1960s and early 1970s;
the 1990s; and the 2000s. These phases coincide with the
arrival of an internationally recognisable conservation ethic
in the 1960s and 1970s, an interest in – and *from* – 'ordi-
nary', marginalised and disenfranchised groups in the 1990s,
and policies of social inclusion and community cohesion in
the 2000s. Our point is that while the heritage sector has
ostensibly mapped the ebb and flow of wider sociological
explorations of community, is has simultaneously absented
itself from more critical explorations of the subject. Consequently, an unchanging and uncritical notion of 'community'
continues to be embedded and disseminated within heritage
policy.

For many commentators, community has become something
of a misnomer: 'a fantasy' (Clarke 2005, cited in Neal & Walters
2008: 280), a 'weasel word' (MacGregor 2001: 188), or something that is tied up with so many ways of thinking about
human relationships that it has come to mean virtually nothing. Like 'identity', the term has become ambiguous and
ambivalent, and can therefore be difficult to use in any mean-

ingful way. An important reason for this is that so much is simply assumed from the word itself that little time has been spent scrutinising and articulating what exactly is meant by 'community', and how it might be recognised within a range of encounters. Indeed, it is a concept that 'needs to be explained rather than *be* the explanation' (Neal and Walters 2008: 281, emphasis added). Important work by authors such as Anderson (1983) Cohen (1985), Bauman (2001) and Amid and Rapport (2002) has provided theoretically engaged work on the issue of community. However, despite this extensive critique – or perhaps because of it – a generic understanding of 'community' continues to dominate public policy.

For Alleyne (2002), this generic understanding has become something of a doxa, or convenience, that tends to refer to rural towns and villages, or, if incorporating the urban context, the working-classes and minority groups. Implicitly, then, the generic conceptualisation of 'community' refers either to social relationships existing 'back in time' or within the strict parameters of social hierarchy. Moreover, as Alleyne (2002: 611) points out, this assumption is based on the premise that the dominant 'we' (read here white, middle- and upper-classes) are 'individuals in society, while they (the Rest) have community (of course, "we" once had community as the dominant form of social organisation, but "we" dropped it on the way to modernity)'. This hierarchical approach has been reiterated by research done by Williams (2003) on UK government policy approaches to community involvement, which tend to denigrate the participatory culture of less affluent wards as 'simple' or 'immature'. As such, this understanding of 'community' is able to weave together an enduring image of tradition, creating a 'golden age of community' (Clarke et al. 2007: 98) that is inevitably tinged with nostalgia, and *applied* by scholars, policymakers and experts to a range of marginalised groups. This idea of 'community' is one commonly associated with the early community studies of the 1950s and 1960s, in which a homogeneous and non-conflictual image of community groups emerged. As such, the accepted notion of 'community' tends to be essentialised and, importantly, comfortable, with positions of power assumed to lie with experts and expertise (Labadi 2007). More often than not, it is also tied up with distinct geographical areas that are rural in character and inevitably romanticised, through which the public are assumed readily to attach ideas of cohesion and inclusion. As Dicks (2000a: 51) points out, it has become coupled with an idealisation of place. Although sociological explorations of the term have moved on significantly from this 'feel-good' factor, a conceptualisation of 'community' as small-scale, face-to-face and attached to place retains a strong political hold, and the heritage sector offers no exception.

The beginnings of a community focus in heritage studies

A focus on 'community' in archaeological and heritage projects was relatively rare before the 1970s (Malloy 2003). Although volunteerism and amateur archaeology have a long history in the UK, as does support for the preservation and conservation of archaeology evidenced by a suite of 'Friends of …' groups, a formal acknowledgement of the lobbying work of a range of interest groups can be pinpointed to the 1970s with the work of *RESCUE: The British Archaeological Trust* (1971), *SAVE Britain's Heritage* (1975), and *The Interpretation of Britain's Heritage* (1975). Similar lobbying also occurred in the US and Australia at this time (see Barthel 1996; Smith 2004a). It is this timeframe that heritage professionals regularly associate with the emergence of a serious public engagement with heritage and archaeology. With the publication of *Public Archaeology* by McGimsey in 1972 and the concerted efforts of Pamela Cressey to introduce the notion of 'community archaeology', the visibility of 'community' was also signalled to be of academic interest, a point that can be illustrated by the emergence of scholarly work such as *Guardians of Community Heritage* (Walker 1984) and *Community Archaeology: A Fieldworker's Handbook of Organization and Techniques* (Liddle 1985).

The emergence of public, academic and political interest in heritage and archaeology is often explained in terms of a wider sense of environmental crisis, at a time when the Western world witnessed massive economic expansion, warnings of global shortages, spectacular nuclear accidents, and a huge growth in urban and rural development. In the UK, this sense of crisis played out in public reactions to the building of large swathes of new motorway, the wiping away of terraced housing and a general sense of being over-awed at large-scale development. This momentum was not confined to the UK, as similar issues were also agitating groups and individuals in many other Western countries. Two responses to this crisis of heritage are relevant here. First, the material culture associated with heritage and archaeology was popularly and politically re-imagined as 'fragile, finite and non-renewable resources'. Debate and discussion of heritage thus focussed not on *what* it might be, but on *how* it ought to be managed. Inevitably, this meant drawing upon the work and advice of particular experts; in this case, the epistemological and ontological frameworks favoured by archaeologists, art historians and architects. Second, the formulation of policies and procedures for the technical management of heritage led to the formalisation of an archaeological profession in the UK (Merriman 2002: 550). One aspect of this was the development of archaeological heritage management (AHM), cultural heritage management (CHM), or cultural resource management (CRM), which was established as a counterpoint to academic archaeology.[2] Imagined as a technical concern bound up with preservation and conservation, CHM ostensibly operated as a mechanism through which archaeology was planned, protected and managed *in the public interest* (Merriman 2004: 3). It was thus with some irony that the vociferous lobbying of volunteer and hobby groups in effect led to decreased amateur and public involvement in archaeological practice (Merriman 2002: 550).

It was also at this time that a particular idea of heritage was naturalised, which works towards sustaining and shaping the parameters of debate around issues of community and public engagement. Legislative documents that embed this idea of heritage in England include the *Ancient Monuments and Archaeological Areas Act 1979*, the *National Heritage Act 1983* and *Planning (Listed Buildings and Conservation Areas) Act 1990*. Smith (2006) has labelled this framing of heritage the Authorised Heritage Discourse (AHD), and has written extensively on both its institutionalisation and its implications (see also Waterton et al. 2006). Within this discourse, emphasis is placed upon the material and tangible which are earmarked as crucial markers of heritage and identity. The importance of this material focus is twofold: first, the above are assumed to provide *real* and tangible reminders of the imaginative bonds used to define and legitimise narratives of the nation; and second, these physical markers justify the prominence of expertise within the particular course of action undertaken to deal with the problem or crisis of heritage that permeated the 1960s and 1970s. The naturalised conservation ethic is thus both technocratic and top-down, designed to deal primarily with a nationally-based understanding of heritage and the past, and draws explicitly on the rights of future generations as a commonsense principle.

The Authorised Heritage Discourse

The roots of the AHD can be traced back to nineteenth-century debates concerned with the authenticity of fabric, and it thus owes its legacy to both Enlightenment rationality and Romanticism. As Ruskin (1849), Morris (1877) and Viollet-le-Duc ([1868] 1990), among others, debated the nature of conservation work and argued for the 'moral' worth of conservation over restoration, ideas about the innate value of fabric became embedded in what was to become standard definitions of 'heritage'. Artistic and aesthetic values were granted primacy, as were authenticity and age, all of which rehearse those ideas associated with Ruskin (1849: 186) and his suggestion that 'the greatest glory of a building is not in its stones, nor in its gold. Its glory is in its Age ...'. Encapsulated within this

assumption of inherent value is the idea of paternalism, permanence and patrimony, out of which a moral sense of obligation emerges that insists that 'we have a duty to champion our
heritage for the enjoyment of future generations' (Green 1996:
1). This ethic was influenced by Ruskin's idea of 'conserve as
found', while Viollet-le-Duc stressed the 'duty' that conserva-
tors had to respect, if not revere, the original meaning and
values of a building. Being 'honest' to the original cultural
meaning of fabric not only reinforces the idea that authenticity
and meaning can only be 'found' in the fabric of places and
objects, it also works to privilege the position of architects,
archaeologists and museum professionals as stewards of that
material culture. This idea of stewardship encompasses the
moral worth of nineteenth-century European debates, and
has come to underpin not only a range of legal heritage instruments (see Smith 2000, 2004a), but also the ethical guidelines
of archaeologists and heritage professionals (see Lynott &
Wylie 2000; World Archaeological Congress 1989, Australian
Archaeological Association 1991, Museums Australia 1999, Canadian Archaeological Association 1997). Although the idea
that material culture has innate meaning and value is questioned today, and has been identified as a problematic legacy of
antiquarianism, it is still a significant assumption, framing the
AHD. However, as Larry Zimmerman (1998, 2000: 72) points
out, the idea of stewardship assumes that only archaeologists
have valid knowledge about the past, and in many respects is a
trope for justifying the existence of heritage professionals, as it
is assumed that they that have the skills to 'unlock' the meaning of the past through its material culture.

The nineteenth century in Europe also saw significant social
changes following the industrial revolution and the rise of
nationalism. A concern to preserve the material culture from
the past was linked not only to an attempt to hold on to familiar
anchors in a changing world, but to modernity's sense that the
present had 'lost' its links to the past (Byrne 2008). A need to
re-forge that link, and to hold onto desired values, helped to
reinforce the AHD's obsession with materiality and monumen-

tality. Material culture makes the intangible and ephemeral *material* – social and cultural values, identity and memories are all intangible and mutable, but are rendered 'real', touchable and in some ways 'knowable' through material symbolism. Monuments, as Choay (2001) points out, act to commemorate or recall those values and meanings important to the present that they hope to see perpetuated in the future.

Thus, in a careful mix of aesthetics, assumptions of innate value, age and authenticity, a particular fascination with the historicity of heritage was formalised. What we are arguing here draws from a critical understanding of discourse and the suggestion that the language we use to talk and think about heritage issues should not be seen as incidental. This is because discourse affects, contributes to, and is constituted by the production and reproduction of social life, including arrangements of power (Richardson 2007: 26). This allows us to think about the AHD as a naturalised discourse working to sustain the privileged positions of a range of experts – along with their interests – while simultaneously thwarting or marginalising the interests of others. This has occurred as a consequence of the systematic uptake of the AHD within national and international policy and practice. As such, the AHD is able to operate from a position of power *because* it legitimises and authorises a particular pattern of management. Our argument borrows from Gramsci's notions of hegemony, and his position that dominant groups will *teach* their values, beliefs and interests to 'the general public' (ibid.: 36). Indeed, if 'education lies at the heart of hegemony', as Richardson (2007: 36) suggests, then the role of expertise within the realm of heritage works to mediate the diffusion and influence of the AHD *through* their pedagogic roles within the management process. Essentially, the AHD is characterised by the privileging of expertise and efficiency. Heritage is imagined as something old, beautiful, tangible and of relevance to the nation, *selected* by experts and *made to matter* (Waterton 2007a: 318). Individuals and interest groups *outside* professionals are rarely acknowledged as playing any sort of active role in the defining, conserving and maintenance of heritage, and are instead characterised as audience, visitor or consumer.

In addition to categories of ownership operating at the level of 'the nation' and 'expertise' are those associated with the middle- and upper-classes; a category that has also played a prominent role in defining the meaning of the terms 'heritage' and 'public' involvement. This involvement can be charted through the role played by the social elite in the activities of the National Trust, and its preservation of particular cultural values represented by the country house, stately home and designed landscape (Smith 2006). This is not an idea of heritage that is capable of sustaining genuine calls for social inclusion and multiculturalism, as it regularly rejects heritage experiences that do not share the same social and cultural markers. Moreover, it asserts that heritage professionals have a duty to educate and inform, thereby ensuring that the cultural symbols of the elite are imparted to, and upheld by, everybody else. A theme linked with this consensual sense of heritage is the idea that it is inherently good, safe and conflict-free, an assumption that provides a powerful underpinning for recent policy emphasis on social inclusion. To make this 'goodliness' work, the AHD not only closes down notions of personal, local and community heritage in an attempt to mitigate conflict and dissent, but also attempts to focus on heritage at a distance, out there or 'back there' in the past (Urry 1996: 148). Paradoxically, then, the AHD attempts to capture all society within a singular understanding of heritage, which is itself a contravention of the term 'inclusion' in that it denies the legitimacy of difference and dissonance. How non-experts are made passive within this scenario is crucial for our discussions of community and/or public engagements with heritage and archaeology. Not only is this promoted by the belief that the proper care of heritage lies with expertise, but also by the associated assumption that identity is inevitably embedded within sites. This lack of a serious examination of precisely *how* identity is tied up with heritage likewise works to flatten out any involvement by non-expert individuals or groups in contemporary society (Waterton 2008a).

'Community' in policy

The conservative nostalgia of 'community' outlined at the beginning of this chapter found congruence with the AHD. Thus, while notions of community have ostensibly found their way into national and international policies, this rhetoric is rarely as engaging in practice. Indeed, accommodation of individuals, communities and public interest groups is more often characterised, as Riley and Harvey (2005: 280) point out, as 'trowel fodder' under 'close guidance' and 'supervision' of a range of experts. This passive role has been embedded within a range of policy frameworks for managing heritage, and its sustained appearance across a range of publications offers the AHD political legitimacy. In England, the 'polluter pays' ethos found in documents such as *Planning Policy Guidance Note 15: Planning and the Historic Environment*, and *Planning Policy Guidance Note 16: Planning and Archaeology*, illustrates the degree to which archaeology was turned into a fully-fledged commercial enterprise. While the developer-led archaeology of the 1990s triggered a recognition of public interest and accountability, this interest was again constructed in terms of outcomes, so that public involvement was imagined either as something *inspired by* archaeological projects or through the provision of information as part of the planning process. With this increasing emphasis on contract archaeology, professionalisation and development controls, community involvement was further marginalised (Carman 2001: 174).

Policy initiatives continue to rehearse the AHD, including *Power of Place: The Future of the Historic Environment* (English Heritage 2000a), *The Historic Environment: A Force for our Future* (DCMS 2001), *The Heritage Protection Review (HPR), Discovering the Past, Shaping the Future* (English Heritage 2005a), *People and Places: Social Inclusion Policy for the Built and Historic Environment* (DCMS 2002), *Conservation*

Principles for the Sustainable Management of the Historic Environment (English Heritage 2006b), and *English Heritage Strategy 2005-2010: Making the Past Part of our Future* (English Heritage 2005b) (Waterton 2007a for a fuller discussion). This range of policy material is particularly significant for discussions of community engagement, as it is through these that notions of 'social inclusion' became embedded within the English heritage sector and the parameters of community participation were formalised. The particular narrative animating this line of policy in the heritage sector revolves around attempts by 'mainstream' heritage organisations to persuade excluded groups to *buy into* and accept dominant understandings of heritage. It is in this context that the notions of 'community' and 'heritage' have found their strongest political backing, as it is *through* heritage that wider goals of creating community cohesion and fostering sustainability are being channelled.

Although our familiarity with this issue lies explicitly with the English experience, it is also one that can be mapped across a range of national experiences, particularly in Europe. The concept itself emerged out of French policy in the 1970s, and since then has spread across the European Union, where it has been taken up by member states in the form of biennial National Action Plans for Social Inclusion (NAPincl) (Koller & Davidson 2008: 307).

Internationally the AHD has also been enshrined in policy and underpins a range of recommendations, charters and conventions. These include documents such as the *Charter for the Restoration of Historic Monuments* (the Athens Charter) 1931 (ICOMOS); the *Convention for the Protection of Cultural Property in the Event of Armed Conflict* (the Hague Convention) 1954 (UNESCO); the *International Charter for the Conservation and Restoration of Monuments and Sites* (the Venice Charter) 1964 (ICOMOS); the *Convention Concerning the Protection of the World Natural and Cultural Heritage* 1972 (UNESCO); the *Charter for the Conservation of Places of Cultural Significance* (the Burra Charter) 1999 (Australian ICOMOS), and the *Convention for the*

1. Heritage, communities and archaeology: a history

Safeguarding of the Intangible Cultural Heritage 2003 (UNESCO), while social inclusion debates have also influenced the last two documents. These texts provide an additional authorising layer to the management of heritage and represent a specific variation of the AHD that also impacts upon the relationships established between community groups.

Collectively, these international documents lay down a straightforward framework for the protection, conservation and restoration of architecture and archaeological sites, within which the scientific nature of preservation is taken as axiomatic. Moreover, they all tend to draw upon, and highlight, the technical expertise of archaeology, art history, architecture and history, and therefore privilege communities of expertise over any other community group. The latter half of the twentieth century thus saw the development of a conservation ethic on an international scale, primarily disseminated through archaeology, art history and architecture. This timeframe highlighted particular elements as important, such as an interest in 'emblems', materiality and fabric. Indeed, as Byrne (1994: 14) argues, the '"authentic" material fabric is valorised by archaeologists and art historians because it constitutes the evidence on which they base their studies; it is valorised by the state because the fabric constitutes the emblem'. Byrne (1991), among other scholars, argues that these notions are inherently Western European, and that UNESCO and ICOMOS, as international representatives of this Western ethos, have established a specific way of seeing heritage as universal.

The nationalistic tendency of Western heritage hit its zenith with the World Heritage Convention, with the idea that there not only is, but only can be, universal value, and that this universal value is best exemplified by European monuments. That the World Heritage List is dominated by the monumental heritage of European states is now acknowledged (Cleere 2001), and indeed the Intangible Cultural Heritage Convention is, in part, an attempt to address that dominance (Aikawa-Faure 2008). However, European dominance of the World Heritage List is no accident, but a direct consequence of Western definitions of heritage and assumptions about innate values. The explicit message passed on by the Convention is clear: *the preservation of this common heritage concerns us all.* In signing or ratifying the Convention, each country gives this sentiment credence. This 'universalising' tendency is an important aspect of the AHD. The universal nature of traditional definitions of heritage lies in the assumption that heritage tells us about the 'human past'. Certainly, heritage *is* something constructed by people, but the values and meanings we give to it are by no means universal in the sense that 'human values' implies. This idea of the universality of both the past and heritage allows experts to speak for the past – because it is a universal past. But *no* heritage site can be regarded as universally valuable or as possessing or symbolising universal meanings. All heritage sites are dissonant and contested (see Chapter 3), and any heritage site, place or object will be valued and understood differently by different individuals, communities or nations. This is a simple observation, underscored by the routine tensions between economic developments, developers, local resident groups and even heritage professionals. It is also evidenced more dramatically in the examples of Seahenge in England, the Ayodhya temple in India, the Bamyan Buddhas in Iran, and may other possible examples. Nonetheless, the simple observation that others value the past differently from ourselves is often forgotten in the universalising rhetoric of the AHD and heritage management practice. The point is that in addition to the formalisation of the AHD at the national level, that discourse was also authorised, safeguarded and naturalised at the international level, as were the cultural values and experiences that underpin it.

As with the emergence of social inclusion policy directives in England, two international documents can be earmarked as reference points within the management process for engaging with communities: the Burra Charter and the Intangible Cultural Heritage Convention. It is in these documents that the term 'community' came to international prominence, with the latter embracing a notion of heritage as 'something shared within and symbolically identified with a cultural community'

34

(Kurin 2004: 69). Both recognise the need to work with and involve people – individuals, community groups and stakeholders – within the processes of managing heritage (Marquis-Kyle & Walker 1992; Blake 2008). Quite what 'community' means in these documents, and what room will be allowed for community decisions or interventions that stand in opposition to those provided by expertise, however, is not so forthcoming. What is clear is that these constructions of 'community' run *parallel* to communities of expertise, which are considered to sit outside – and above – other communities. In short, heritage became something that was done *for* communities and the public, rather than something that was done *with* them.

A more critical 'community' agenda

Loosely since the 1980s, and more vehemently since the 2000s, heritage studies and archaeology have begun to respond to the 'community' agenda emanating from Indigenous and non-Western cultural contexts, and to address issues of ethics, politics, power and the marginalisation of non-Western terms of knowledge. This engagement with shifting boundaries between archaeologists and descendant/Indigenous communities has had a profound impact on the practices of both heritage and archaeology in post-colonial nations (Colwell-Chanthaphonh & Ferguson 2004: 5; Geurds 2007). These groups also began to challenge and contest the very idea of heritage embedded in legislation. In these contexts, relationships between community groups and archaeological practitioners are still haunted by a history of tension and distrust. The 1980s and early 1990s saw particularly vociferous and powerful statements emerging from Indigenous people dissatisfied with the uneven power relationships sustained by policy and legislation (e.g. Langford 1983; Deloria 1992). In particular, these groups sought to challenge the definition of their heritage as an archaeological resource or possession of the national or international community. Although these debates continue, they have succeeded in drawing attention to the deeply entrenched power relations attached to notions of 'science' and 'expertise', which have for so long mediated heritage issues. While these challenges have primarily been characterised as specific to issues of repatriation, illicit trade and reburial debates, there are wider issues to be drawn out that touch upon the affective and emotive dimensions of community heritage (see Chapters 2, 4).

Our argument is that these shifts need not be restricted to what has been termed 'Indigenous archaeology', but may offer lessons for a wider range of community groups seeking greater control and acknowledgment of their definitions, understandings and uses of heritage. The recent history of agitation from a range of non-Western interest groups has undoubtedly spurred a recognition of the need to go beyond uncritical notions of the term 'community' and acknowledge that it is a contested concept, often drawn upon in forms of political resistance (see Chapter 4). While this increased visibility is most often associated with disempowered and displaced groups, it applies also to those who have been marginalised, historically, from the process of 'heritagisation' (Dicks 2003: 140). No longer are individuals, community groups and stakeholders simply supportive of preservation and conservation; they instead seek to have their own sense of heritage acknowledged and legitimised. The secondary committees operating at the international level, along with the wider role of expertise that developed in the 1960s, have since come under sustained criticism by those striving to achieve greater democratisation (Cressey et al. 2003: 3). Despite increased pressure for community involvement, there is, nonetheless, a distinct one-sidedness to how this is carried out in practice, relegated as it is to the 'secondary' issues of methodology and ethics (Moser et al. 2002: 223). 'Public archaeology' and 'public history', as Smith (2007) has pointed out, are still considered to lie outside the more rigorous academic pursuits of 'straight' archaeology and history.

Recently, academic inquiry has sought to rethink 'community' in response to a general dissatisfaction with the term and its unreflective use – although it is important to note that this

shift has not been so forthcoming in a policy sense (Day &
Murdoch 1993; Cooper 2008). It is thus once more a subject
recognised as worthy of academic investigation, particularly as
a response to the reified notion of 'community' most often
found embedded in archaeological practices and public policy. As such, a large amount of research has recently been
conducted – both within and outside heritage studies – that
has worked to redefine community as something that is
(re)constructed within ongoing experiences, engagements and
relations between a range of people, sometimes consensually
and sometimes contentiously (Alleyne 2002: 608). It is thus a
term or entity that is created and constituted in *action* and in
the present (ibid.). Indeed, as Dicks (2000a: 97) points out, a
community is often constructed, produced and maintained
through its heritage work, and incorporates the very active
concerns, tensions and anxieties that drive community projects
in the first place. Together, these influences have triggered a
broadening of 'the imagined community' (Anderson 1983) from
'the nation' to a range of geographical, social, ethnic and cultural
sub-groups, including those held together by virtual social networking (see Chapter 6). This decoupling of 'community' from
geography has also been accompanied by the recognition that it is
saturated with power, and is thus an inevitably dissonant and
contested term (Hoggett 1997: 14). Not only, then, do we need to
move away from the assumption that all community groups are
similar and defined by ethnic or socio-economic classifications, we
also need actively to acknowledge that power and empowerment
are not neutral or uniformly distributed within any given community. The issue, as Green et al. (2003: 382) point out, is that an
'entire community cannot be empowered simultaneously; certain
individuals will be more empowered than others, with the impli-
cation that empowerment activities alter the social landscape'.
Our re-theorisation of community needs to acknowledge, to quote
Thrift (2005: 139-40), that:

> achieving sociality does not mean that everything has to
> be rosy ... sociality does not have to be the same thing as

liking others. It includes all kinds of acts of kindness and compassion, certainly, but equally there are all signs of active dislike being actively pursued ... as malign gossip, endless complaint, the full spectrum of jealousy, petty snobbery, personal deprecation, pointless authoritarianism, various forms of schadenfreude, and all the other ritual pleasures of everyday life ... It is to say, however, that we need to think more carefully about whether we really have it in us to just be unalloyedly nice to others at all times in every single place: most situations can and do bring forth both nice and nasty.

This means that we have to move away from uncritical and dialogically closed relationships with community groups and reconsider the nature of involvement, responsibility and control. This takes us beyond the hierarchical levels of involvement proposed by Moser et al. (2002), towards a framework of engagement that is no longer guided by the dominant understanding of heritage and its management. This means we have to deal with power and the consequences of alienation. Acknowledging these deeply entrenched relations of power requires a total reconsideration of the conventional relationships assumed between community groups and archaeologists, of whom the latter are presumed to exist *outside* the boundaries of 'community'. However, for the purposes of this volume, archaeology is re-imagined as precisely that – another community group bound by common interests. As Nicholas and Hollowell (2007) point out, this requires a leap forward in terms of power, particularly in relation to scholarly privilege and control. The intent is to make processes of managing heritage less patronising and paternalistic, and more open to self-examination, critical reflection and negotiation. Importantly, it means abandoning the notion that we are 'discovering the truth' on behalf of 'everyone'.

Conclusion

The idea of 'community' embedded in public policy remains uncritically 'positive', 'comfortable' and traditional, but a pivotal point within current negotiations around social exclusion, multiculturalism and cultural diversity. As a central plank of government, it has spread across associated departments, where it has become a tool with the implicit aim of engendering consensus. Here, 'community' is used in association with popular discourses drawn upon to divide the nation between the majority, the white middle-classes, and various minority/ethnic/excluded communities as a mechanism of government (Alleyne 2002: 609). Such is the degree of naturalisation of the white middle-classes that as a socio-economic group they are rendered invisible and thus are not considered to 'have community or ethnic identity in the same way as everybody else, whiteness being the norm' (ibid.: 609). This same argument can be applied to communities of expertise, which are likewise imagined to operate outside the parameters set in place for 'community' involvement and participation in decision-making. Following this, as Alexander (2007) argues, white groups and professionals are rarely targeted as the problem as it is the cultural values of excluded groups that become the focus of social reform. This harnessing of 'community' to wider constructions of artificial harmony is assimilatory, in that it works to regulate and integrate various excluded communities through an enforced adherence to a particular set of national values or 'norms of acceptability' (Alexander 2007: 116; Wetherell 2007: 8). The notion of community, in this instance, is forced to play a dual role that is both positive – in terms of the 'ideal' that policy aspires to – and negative – in terms of the *wrong* kind of community encountered within minority and excluded groups (Alexander 2007: 121). Despite a significant increase in popular, political and academic interest in community participation, involvement and identity, the idea of community continues to revolve around a self-evident and homogeneous understanding that is itself an obstacle. It is also something that is attended to on a case-by-case basis, rather than holistically embedded across the management process. As such, it is important to remind ourselves, as Brent (1997: 82) points out, that 'community is not a term suitable for use as a unequivocal slogan of redemption'.

2

Material culture, memory and identity

Introduction

What lies at the heart of the uneasy relationship between communities in general and the community of heritage professionals is the idea of heritage. How it is defined, what is done with it, and the uses it is put to are the pivotal points from which tensions, misunderstandings and conflicts arise. This chapter argues that there is a significant disjunction between authorised, professional and institutional understandings or definitions of heritage and the realities or material consequences that heritage has. That is, heritage does social, political and cultural 'work' in society, but definitions of heritage at large in public policy, legal instruments and management practices fail to acknowledge this. While they gesture at acknowledging that heritage has an integral link with identity, authorised or traditional definitions do not actually *understand* this link in any meaningful way. This chapter critically develops a definition of heritage that actively incorporates the linkages between material culture, memory and identity. The ways in which communities utilise heritage are identified and the disjunction between this use and professional definitions is highlighted. From this, the consequences of heritage knowledge and practice are identified and explored.

Heritage as a known thing?

In archaeological terms, heritage is often understood to be the material culture of the past, or all those artefacts and structures produced by humans that make up the archaeological record and are used to explain, or help explain, the past – heritage is a known thing. For some archaeologists, heritage and archaeological material culture are one and the same thing; and that is the data that helps to define both the past and who 'we' *are* in the present. Although there is explicit recognition in the literature that such interpretations of the past are neither definitive nor objective, there is often a tacit assumption that the knowledge produced by the discipline informs 'identity' and is thus 'heritage'. This assumption survives even though archaeologists recognise the multi-vocality of interpretations of the past, and is particularly strong in Europe, and in archaeological dealings with non-Indigenous pasts and communities in the ex-colonial countries of North America and Australasia. Indeed, so strong is this assumption that archaeologists – and archaeological knowledge – often form the primary body of expertise (followed, perhaps, by architecture) drawn upon in the development of heritage management practices. Archaeologists readily find employment as heritage practitioners in key government heritage agencies, inter-government heritage organisations, heritage amenity societies and other NGOs, or they work as freelance consultants within units, or other private/semi-private organisations involved in the environmental assessment process. This assumed synergy between 'heritage' and 'archaeological data' can be summed up in Britain with reference to the popularity of the term 'Archaeological Heritage Management'.

This materiality of archaeological data makes the concept of heritage (and, by inference, ideas of 'identity' deemed to be linked to heritage) inherently *knowable*. The way in which archaeological heritage can be discovered, defined (spatially and conceptually), recorded, mapped, put on a site register or any other list, and finally, managed and conserved, makes heritage both knowable and controllable. The sense that heritage is a known thing is also reinforced by the naturalisation of archaeological assumptions about heritage in legal and policy instruments. As much as heritage is knowable by archaeologists, it is also a known thing for heritage practitioners more generally, simply because it is defined in national and international legal and policy documents. However, this close linkage of archaeological material culture and heritage is problematic and has led to the conflation of heritage with archaeological data and knowledge. This conflation of archaeological data, and material culture more generally, with heritage underwrites the misunderstandings and tensions between archaeologists and many other communities. This is because heritage is *not* a known thing – nor is it a thing at all. Rather, it is mutable and intangible and means many different things to many different people and communities.

Smith's notion of the AHD, as developed in Chapter 1, goes some way towards explaining this propensity to equate 'heritage' with 'archaeological data', as it is a discourse that works to define both the concept of heritage and the boundaries of debates about its nature, values and meanings. These boundaries are very much guided by the discourse's historical associations with archaeology. What is significant about this discourse is its near complete naturalisation, as it is from this position that the AHD is able to promote and maintain social inequalities. While the extent to which the AHD underpins heritage policy and practice has already been discussed, it remains crucial for understanding the misunderstandings and tensions between various communities and groups, including communities of archaeological and other heritage professionals. The AHD works to appropriate, obscure or misrecognise the heritage values and knowledge that communities have of the past. Moreover, heritage professionals assume a role as spokespeople and *educators* for the past and thus community heritage, not only because they are stewards for the past, but because it is 'the past' – singular – and the past belongs to all of humanity. Thus, community heritage will never, in terms of the hierarchy of values constructed by the AHD, be as important or as representative as 'national' heritage, and consequently is devalued or ignored.

Rethinking heritage

The re-theorisation of heritage adopted here emerges out of Smith's (2006) idea that heritage is a cultural process or performance of meaning-making. Heritage, therefore, becomes not a thing or a place, but an intangible process in which social and cultural values are identified, negotiated, rejected or affirmed. It is thus what is done at, or with, heritage sites that is significant, rather than the places themselves. As Smith states:

> There is no one defining action or moment of heritage, but rather a range of activities that include remembering, commemoration, communicating and passing on knowledge and memories, asserting and expressing identity and social and cultural values and meanings. As an experience, and as a social and cultural performance, it is something with which people actively, often self-consciously, and critically engage in ... The product or the consequences of heritage activities are the emotions and experiences and the memories of them that they create (ibid.: 83).

The memories and experiences created and reinforced by heritage performances help bind communities and other social and cultural groups through the creation of shared experiences, values and memories, all of which work to help cement or recreate social networks and ties. This definition of heritage draws on Samuel's (1994) notion of 'theatres of memory', through which 'place' becomes a locus for performing, mediating and negotiating the meaning of the past for the present. It also draws on similar work by Dicks (2000b) and her suggestion that heritage is an act of communication, and that of Harvey (2001), who argues that heritage is a 'verb' rather than

44

a noun. This idea also underpins the work of Kirshenblatt-Gimblett (1998), Byrne (2008) and Bendix (2008), and informs their explorations of how concepts of heritage or material culture are used to legitimise, or make material, the intangibilities of culture and human experience. The idea of heritage as a cultural process is important as it allows for a broader capacity within which to consider how and why a variety of things can become heritage or, conversely, cease to be heritage. This definition of heritage does not negate traditional arguments about the importance of identity-making. Rather, it sees this process as ultimately more fluid and changeable than identifying heritage as a 'thing' or place allows.

Memory and identity: the emotive nature of heritage

Memory and identity are fluid, intangible and inherently social concepts. Recollection, reminiscing and remembering – either in formal ceremonies of commemoration or in day-to-day activities – are social activities (Connerton 1991). The way societies or other collectives choose to remember and reminisce, and what they choose to remember and forget, are thus cultural and social processes of meaning-making. Further, any single event can be remembered differently and made meaningful or non-meaningful by different individuals and communities.

A case in point is the cultural phenomenon of Holocaust remembering, which has been memorialised in dispersed and diverse ways, internationally, nationally and sub-nationally. This has occurred through a range of Holocaust Memorial Days undertaken by at least fourteen countries, all of which are negotiating as much a process of national forgetting as of national remembering (Yuval-Davis & Silverman 2002). For Britain, this form of national remembering involves a process of obfuscation that subtly forgets anti-Semitism and complacency during the Second World War (ibid.: 116). In their examination of cosmopolitan memory formations in Israel, Germany and the USA, Levy and Sznaider (2002) note that different collective memories are drawn upon to represent and mediate the same difficult past for different communities. For Israel, this oscillates between silenced, painful memories and sacred remembrance (ibid.: 94). In Germany, the immediate silences of the post-war years have been replaced by a more self-critical national narrative of the nation's past (Huyssen 1995: 257), while the USA has performed its own unique memorialisation, referred to as the 'Americanisation of the Holocaust', which remembers the American nation as 'the primary keepers of the flame of remembrance' (Shandler 1999; Levy & Sznaider 2002: 98). At the same time, sub-national processes *within* each country present alternative memories or ways of remembering. Further, these debates reflect upon the iconic status granted to the historical reality of Auschwitz as an emblem of the Holocaust, rendering it a monument whose memories are under dispute (Yuval-Davis & Silverman 2002: 111) (Figure 2.1).

In the case of the Warsaw Ghetto Monument, the monument evokes different memories for different viewers, as a site of resistance, a memory to suffering and mythic memory of heroism (Young 1989). Moreover, as different political groups and communities undertake different performances of commemoration at and around the monument they rehearse and make new meanings for themselves. The point is that memory cannot be understood as something that is simply passed on, unchanged, from generation to generation, nor is it a 'thing' to have and catalogue. Indeed, no form of memory, collective or otherwise, will cease to be contingent and unstable despite international appeals to its intractability and permanence (Huyssen 1995: 249). Rather, memories are recast and recreated in the minds of each generation to help them make sense of the present and, in the process, come to understand themselves (ibid.: 90). Even the immediate recollections of individuals, whether they are of private and family events or as eye-witnesses to historic moments, will be reinterpreted and thus remade and re-understood in the context of present day experiences and the aspirations and desires of those doing the remembering (Wertsch 2002).

This fluidity of memory is something that challenges us. It is

2.1. The main entrance to Auschwitz II-Birkenau, Poland. The railway tracks that transported prisoners from across German-occupied Europe to the concentration and extermination camp (1940-45) are still visible. It now forms part of the Auschwitz-Birkenau State Museum and was inscribed on UNESCO's World Heritage List in 1979. [Photo: E. Waterton]

much easier to accept the authority of the written text and the intellectual authority of historians and archaeologists when dealing with collective memories or recounting pasts to which we were not witness. Moreover, there is no spontaneous memory. Memories need to be actively remembered, and thus memory needs to take root in the concrete object or site, and needs to be maintained through anniversaries or celebrations, otherwise it becomes overtaken by, or lost in, the authority held by universal claims of history (Nora 1989: 9-12). Monuments, and material culture more generally, act as cultural tools in the processes of remembering and forgetting (Wersch 2002). Indeed, heritage works to help 'organise' public and historical memory (Young 1989: 101). Further, memories are also recalled in the 'doing' (Crouch & Parker 2003: 396), and both the commemorations society organises around monuments and the practices of heritage management are actions involved in the creation and maintenance of collective memories.

Memory underpins identity, and different communities or collectives will have different mnemonic strategies they draw upon to help them reinforce their sense of self and collective identity (Misztal 2003: 15). Identity, like memory, is also intangible and fluid, such that none of us will possess a single 'identity'. Rather, our sense of self is composed of many different, although often overlapping and interlinked, social identities, which are forged not only in terms of 'who we are', but also of 'who we are not'. As with memory, linking identity to physical places and objects renders the intangible *material* and gives it physical 'reality' (Graham et al. 2000). Further, anchoring identity to material culture and places makes the mapping of our own individual or collective identities more manageable and comprehensible. This is a point illustrated by mural paintings of the Somme in Northern Ireland, which act as visual *aides-memoire* for a range of commemorative processes and objectified reminders of disparate Northern Irish identities (Jarman 1999: 184). Images of the Battle of the Somme and the 36th Division are tangible manifestations of a complex and contested process of identity construction within Ulster, which attempts to negotiate, as Graham and Shirlow (2002) argue, a range of identities including those associated with paramilitary legitimisation, protestant working-class identities and prospects for reconciliation. While the images contained within murals more generally are varied, as are the messages they contain, they nonetheless perform a role in constructions – and maintenance – of community identity (Graham 1998).

These links between identity and heritage are well documented in the literature, and its symbolic value is not in dispute here; the point is the emotive nature of heritage. Identity and memory are not simply something you 'have', but are something you experience and perform. Heritage, then, does not just simply sit there and proclaim the viewer's identity. Rather, viewers must emotionally engage with heritage, and meaningfully interact with it, for that site or place to 'speak to' the individual. Indeed, it is in a mix of doing, reacting, feeling and understanding that heritage is created, as part of a wider cultural process within which people ascertain feelings of connection, belonging and a sense of themselves. Poria et al. (2003), in their study of the behaviour of domestic and international visitors to the Wailing Wall in Jerusalem, make a similar observation in their conclusion that people come to heritage sites not just to 'gaze' but also to 'feel'. The emotional quality of heritage is thus not abstract, but is *felt* and continually reinforced and remade in the performances of heritage; that is, it is continually *experienced* and *re-experienced* at and through the performances of heritage.

Memories and people's sense of self and belonging – their sense of identity – are highly emotive constructs. This is, of course, obvious and may appear to be hardly worth stating. However, the emotional quality of heritage is often like 'an elephant in the room'; we all know it is there but it can be seen as quite embarrassing, especially if it is linked to expressions of nationalism or patriotism, and so it often goes unaddressed. Further, the emotional quality of heritage is often tacitly assumed to be positive, as heritage is meant to provide a comfortable and comforting affirmation of 'who we are' – after all, as constructed within the AHD, heritage is 'good', 'great' and 'consensual'. However, with the creation of any sense of inclusion comes, inevitably, exclusion, and the emotions that heritage generates can be as negative as they can be positive. With places or heritage that acknowledge the traumatic aspects of a community's or culture's past – sites of dissonance, shame or pain – the emotions and memories evoked can be painful or mixed (Tunbridge & Ashworth 1996; Logan & Reeves 2008). Linkon and Russo's (2002) study of the way industrial workers in the deindustrialised town of Youngstown in the USA sought to renegotiate their sense of identity is a case in point. The past of Youngstown is both painful in terms of the brutalities of working-class history, but also a source of pride in terms of community solidarity and achievements. The challenge is negotiating new identity(ies) that incorporate both the bad and the good as the Youngstown communities attempt to recreate themselves in the context of deindustrialisation (ibid: 245).

The complexity of the emotional quality of heritage can also be witnessed in the religious and spiritual values it is given. Heritage does not just represent or symbolise established religious identities and beliefs, but can also take on spiritual values for other communities. This can be observed in the conflicts in England over pagan access to sites such as Stonehenge and Seahenge (Skeates 2000). As Byrne et al. (2006) point out, this aspect of community connection is often underplayed in the West because of what they label a 'secularity premise' in dominant approaches to heritage management. They argue that an array of deeply emotive and abiding spiritual affinities and responses emerge from our associations with heritage places, sites and landscapes. Their analysis of enchanted parklands documents the range of spiritual meanings given to landscapes around Sydney, Australia, by a range of community groups, as well as by established religious communities. Their contention is that while this aspect of emotional connection often falls below the threshold of conventional heritage evaluations, and thus remains invisible in a management sense, it is nonetheless a valid projection of meaning onto a landscape.

Our acknowledgment of the emotional qualities of heritage is important for the observations it enables us to make about the cultural process of heritage itself. This is because our emotional connections to heritage experiences are inevitably managed and open to interventions through the way heritage places organise and facilitate remembering and expressions of identity. Heritage sites are points at which our sense of place becomes anchored and emotionally manageable. Those experiences of memory-making, remembering and other forms of emotional identity expression are made manageable by taking them out of the 'everyday' and concentrating them in specific performances in which 'heritage' places are identified, looked after and visited. This process is done at both national and community levels. Although the national process is called heritage management, and is governed by national legislation and public policies, it is nonetheless part of the process in which the emotional registers of national and collective identities, and processes of remembering and commemoration, are regulated and controlled.

The difficulties between communities occur as a consequence of the extent to which the emotional quality of heritage goes unacknowledged. More specifically, they are a symptom of the ways in which our emotional connections are managed and regulated through the privileged position of the heritage management process as opposed to other forms of heritage engagement. Nostalgia is an important issue here. Wright (1985) and Hewison (1987), in particular, have criticised the so-called 'heritage industry' (that is, heritage tourism) for creating sanitised and historically inauthentic versions of the past. In so doing, both have dismissed the emotional quality of heritage as nostalgia. While they make a valid point – that certain heritage interpretations and performances can create or legitimise reactionary nostalgic heritage performances – their concern over nostalgia has become a dominant theme in contemporary heritage debates in the West. In England, at least, there is a tendency to dismiss or equate the full emotional register of heritage with 'nostalgia', along with all the negative connotations of sanitisation and reactionary visions of the past that this entails. However, as Strangleman (1999) argues, nostalgia is often confused with memory. Indeed, discourses of nostalgia are often used to dismiss or debase the rememberings of communities and individuals whose heritage and sense of identity exist outside the dominant narratives of national heritage: nations remember, communities reminisce; national heritage constructs national identity, community heritage is nostalgic. This tendency is reinforced by the generic conceptualisation of 'community' that operates within the policy sphere discussed in Chapter 1, which is itself tied up with images of either 'tradition' and a rural 'golden age', or strict parameters of social hierarchy in which only the non-white and non-upper to middle-classes have community. In this structuring, the nostalgia of communities and their rememberings is taken as self-evident. A hierarchy of heritage, then, is not only constructed by the AHD, where national heritage is valued more than sub-national or community heritage, but is reinforced by wider political assumptions of who can – and cannot – form part of a 'community'.

One of the issues that heritage professionals have commonly commented on to us, and often with some bemusement, is the emotional response of communities not only to their heritage, but to external attempts to manage that heritage. This bemusement derives from the extent to which we work within the AHD, which obscures and ignores the emotional quality of heritage and all that means for an individual's and community's sense of place. This compartmentalisation of 'experts' from 'communities' also spills out semantically where it forms part of the way in which institutions and professionals talk and write about engagements with heritage. Here, communities are characterised as those that 'feel', whereas experts are those who 'think' and 'know' in a process that skilfully 'avoids' subjectivities (for an example of this in action see Clark 2006: 97). The emotional response of communities is thus often fuelled by frustration; a frustration that also often works to mask more complex and nuanced emotional responses from the heritage expert. This frustration can arise for a range of reasons, such as: the lack of recognition given to their heritage; 'talking past' experts about the nature and meaning of heritage; finding their heritage intensely personal and emotional, and seeing those emotions either disregarded or misinterpreted. These frustrations also mount when the emotional elements of heritage become the subject of 'management', and thus of interventions by expertise and heritage agencies – individuals and organisations that could not possibly have the same emotional linkage or understanding of the heritage in question as community members.

These interventions inevitably work to disregard those emotions without necessarily meaning to do so.

Conclusion: the arenas of conflict

Mapping the potential arenas of conflict around issues of heritage for community groups is a complex task. This is heightened by the fluidity of communities and the fact that no community is itself homogeneous and self-referential. Tensions more often than not exist between a range of heritage professionals and community groups, no matter what their nature. Even when there are apparently harmonious working relationships, the room for misunderstanding is always there and tensions arise not only from the differing aspirations and agendas of community groups but from the definitions of heritage each group employs. For archaeologists, heritage is data. As such, it offers them a convincing way of knowing and understanding the past. It is the material reason for the existence of the discipline. As Julie Lahn (1996) notes, the possession of certain prestigious objects or data sets by individuals, and indeed collectively by the discipline, is symbolic of the community identity claims made by archaeologists. This understanding of heritage is entirely cognisant with the way we have been arguing heritage is used by communities. For communities too, heritage is about knowing the past through remembering and commemoration, and through the performances of identity creation and recreation. However, for both archaeologists and communities these performances are often masked by the AHD. Archaeologists often remain unaware of the heritage value the data they collect carries for themselves and the consequences of their knowledge for community self-awareness and pride. Moreover, they remain unaware of the power this gives them in terms of their ability to make claims about community 'involvement' and 'participation' without putting in jeopardy their rights of access and control as cultural experts and custodians. Communities construct a sense of heritage that they know may never be regarded as important or relevant; they may not even recognise that a community heritage exists simply because that heritage is not recognised within the authorising agencies of the dominant heritage discourse. The AHD can work equally to mask the role and nature of heritage within and from communities as it does from archaeologists. The possibilities for conflict are endless as the AHD masks the consequences of heritage. The ability of the AHD to render heritage as a thing to be 'managed' means that the emotional and political work that heritage does in our society goes unrecognised and can lead to frustrating bewilderment as communities and the community of expertise talk past one another and misunderstand the impact each has on the other.

3

Community dissonance

Introduction

In the Introduction to the edited volume *Public Archaeology*, Nick Merriman (2004: 4) remarked that 'most of the public aspects of archaeology are about conflict, or what Tunbridge and Ashworth (1996) have called "dissonant heritage" '. The AHD typically assumes that heritage is good, safe and consensual. Yet, if we accept that contemporary societies are diverse and conflict-ridden, it would probably be fair to say that the heritage drawn upon and used by each individual and pocket of society is itself variable and defined in its own terms (Bonnell & Simon 2007: 65). The idea, then, that everyone's idea of heritage will be 'good', 'safe' and meaningful *for everyone else* seems naïve, if not impossible. It is also an idea that carries significant implications – or impediments – for community groups attempting to define and assert a sense of heritage that is *not* always consensual, 'good' and 'safe'.

Difficult histories

In *The Guilt of Nations: Restitution and Negotiating Historical Injustices*, Elazar Barkan (2000) draws attention to the prominence of 'moral issues' in the current international arena, prompting what could be labelled a national self-reflexivity. From the 1990s onwards, Barkan argues, international and national politics have taken up an interest in dark histories, an interest that has been used to rewrite national memories and identities with a strong rhetoric of human rights and cultural pluralism. Those difficult histories include: the Holocaust; the

bombing of Hiroshima and Nagasaki; the exploitation and enslavement of African peoples; the sexual servitude of 'enemy'
women by Japan in the Second World War; Australia's Stolen
Generations; and the United States' role in backing counter-
terrorism campaigns in Guatemala, among others. The willingness of various heritage institutions to engage with these
disparate and often hidden narratives of the past varies, but
there is, as Kirshenblatt-Gimblett (2000, cited in Bonnell &
Simon 2007: 65) points out, an overarching opening up of museums and heritage centres to the 'darker side of human society'. It is this type of negative heritage that forms a significant
part of Tunbridge and Ashworth's (1996) volume, *Dissonant
Heritage: The Management of the Past as a Resource in Conflict*, as histories that are 'particularly prone to dissonance'
(Ashworth 2002). Negative heritage can be understood as:
'dark tourism', or 'actual or symbolic encounters with death'
(Seaton 1999: 131); 'atrocity sites' such as Hiroshima and the
Killing Fields; 'disaster sites' such as Pompeii; 'celebrity
deaths' such as those sites associated with the assassinations
of John F. Kennedy and John Lennon; 'battlefields' such as
Waterloo; 'prison heritage' such as Robben Island; and 'memorials' such as war graves, catacombs and graveyards (ibid.: 131;
Ashworth 2008; Logan & Reeves 2008).

This opening up of dark or difficult histories is not limited to
large-scale political acts of remembrance or academic interests,
but has itself become a potent part of the tourism industry,
with some 700,000 people visiting Auschwitz-Birkenau concentration camp each year (see Figure 2.1). This is also evidenced
by the recent emergence of tourism sites on the internet such
as *Grief Tourism*[1] and the *Dark Tourism Forum*,[2] and the
introduction of the terms 'the grief tourist' and 'thanatourism'.
While we do not limit our understanding of dissonance to these
ideas of 'dark' or 'painful' histories, it is nonetheless a useful
place to start.

For Tunbridge and Ashworth (1996: 21), heritage is inherently conflictual, and will result in inevitable tensions,
disharmonies, discordances or lack of agreement – whether

latent or active – each time we engage with it, albeit to a varying degree. This notion rests on the idea that:

> If all heritage is someone's heritage and therefore logi-cally not someone else's, any creation of heritage from the past disinherits someone completely or partially (Ash-worth 2002: 363).

We would go a little further and suggest that all heritage is multi-faceted, multi-sensual and multi-emotive, with each ex-perience and encounter prompting an array of interpretations, perspectives and responses that both collide and compete. This is a condition of heritage whether at a tourist destination, as a marketing product, a local amenity, a national focal point, a museum's message or a community's experience. In short, dis-sonance will always occur. It may be a mild undercurrent, or it may be politically, socially and ethically fraught, and this will depend on not only how each different group and community attempts to validate its own sense of heritage, but also how that sense of heritage is received and understood by alternative groups and communities. How it will be greeted is never cer-tain, as each response will shift between agreement, indiffer-ence and outright hostility, but what Tunbridge and Ashworth suggest *will* be certain is the creation of dissonance *each time* something is named, or selected, as 'heritage'. This is because one perspective or understanding of heritage will inevitably become the version that has behind it the power to make it matter (Hall 1999). Consequently, a range of alternative per-spectives will be marginalised, discounted or ignored, and are ultimately, as Tunbridge and Ashworth (1996: 30; see also Teye & Timothy 2004: 149) argue, disinherited. Thus the process of naming – and the process of possessing and regulating – heritage will always be inflected with power and dissonance. Moreover, as Smith (2006) points out, it will always be political.

For the most part, Tunbridge and Ashworth are concerned with the interpretation of heritage, listing a range of contexts – social, cultural, economic and political – within which disso-

nance will arise, and drawing out the implications each interpretation may have for issues of class, gender, religion, persons
with disabilities, ethnicity and sexuality. This discordance, or
dissonance, however, does not simply occur as a consequence of
interpretation. Rather, it occurs in the very act of defining and
ascribing meaning to heritage. Notions of ideology and hegemony are thus instrumental to this discussion, as any negotiation
with heritage – and thus any instance of dissonance – takes place
within a wider social and political context that is itself cut
through with uneven relations of power, both hidden and explicit.
The very act of naming something 'heritage' is mediated by these
structures of power, which will themselves regulate the responsiveness of others to that act of naming. Thus, while everybody
'has a right to' their heritage, it is invariably competitive and
appropriating, and thus not so straightforward.

As a companion piece to Tunbridge and Ashworth, Bonnell
and Roger (2007) explore what they term 'difficult exhibitions'.
Falling within this category is the attempted *Enola Gay* exhibition at the Smithsonian Air and Space Museum, which sought
to display the plane that carried and dropped the atomic bomb
'little boy' on Hiroshima on 6 August 1945. This display of the
restored B-29 'superfortress', *Enola Gay*, resulted in protests
and dissension from a range of interest groups, the cancellation
of the exhibition, and the eventual resignation of the museum's
director, all of which took place between 1993 and 1995 (Zolberg 1998; Gieryn 1998; Dickenson 2006: 26). The original
Smithsonian exhibition, with its focus upon 'morality' and 'ne-
cessity', was an explicit attempt to problematise the past and
incite emotional and conflicting responses (Wallace 1996: 273).
In particular, the exhibition script attempted to question the
dominant, and justificatory, storyline that the detonation of the
atomic bombs 'saved a million American lives' (Kishimoto 2004:
20). In this aim, the curators self-consciously attempted to
sponsor complex and critical reflection concerned with war and
racism (Zolberg 1998: 565), thereby tackling dissonance front
on; but it was not without its problems – many of which the
museum curators did not see coming.

3. Community dissonance

First, the Smithsonian questioned the accuracy of estimates for the number of potential American causalities should the war have continued, which were used to inform the decision to unleash the bomb. This line of questioning saw the Smithsonian Institute charged with rendering America's decision immoral (Wallace 1996: 273). US veteran groups, in particular, took offence, as they had hoped that the exhibition would represent 'a tribute to the bravery of their comrades' (Zolberg 1998: 575). In contrast, anti-war activists and peace organisations threatened to protest against any attempt by the museum to *downplay* the number of deaths and causalities resulting from the bombs dropped on Japan. The controversy involved not only historians both within and outside the Smithsonian, but also the Air Force Association, the American Legion, the pilot of the *Enola Gay*, peace groups, anti-nuclear groups and a range of politicians. It also prompted a member of the US House of Representatives to conclude that Americans 'want the Smithsonian to reflect real America and not something that a historian dreamed up' (quoted in Dickenson 2006: 26), and should be something that avoids 'impugning the memory of those who gave their lives for freedom' (Senate Resolution 1994, quoted in Beazley 2007: 44). These groups engaged in a two-year long debate that, while ostensibly revolving around the specific exhibition of the *Enola Gay*, was concerned with wider issues of collective memory and how the past should be remembered. While a smaller exhibition did eventually take place in 1995, this focussed primarily upon the plane itself in terms of its capabilities and restoration. Details were also provided of its mission, although no mention was made of the impact the bombing had on the population of Japan. For Wallace (1996: 285) one of the most significant problems underpinning this controversy was the failure of the Smithsonian to comprehend its stakeholders, and its consequent neglect of interested communities and who should speak for them.

Although the example of the *Enola Gay* controversy is an extreme case – at least in terms of the media attention gained and the heat generated by the conflict – it is a useful reminder of what is at stake for communities and why heritage professionals often come into conflict. How heritage and history is interpreted and defined will have consequences for someone's sense of place and identity. Understanding the emotional and political investment communities have in their identities is paramount in working with such groups. It is also vital to comprehend how the identities and historical narratives valued by one community interact with other communities or wider social and political public debates. The *Enola Gay* conflict was about whose version of history – and thus whose morality and values – should be given legitimacy and whose should not. The wider consequence of the interplay between the communities involved and the museum staff inevitably resulted in one community's sense of history, and the social values they drew from it, being privileged while another's was de-privileged, even marginalised. Further, this conflict, like most conflicts and negotiations between communities and heritage professionals, operated against the wider backdrop of public debate, as it also engaged with articulating how America as a nation and Americans as a people saw themselves. Understanding the wider networks of meaning-making that heritage becomes embroiled in – or is in fact already a part of – will not necessarily mean that heritage professionals can and will avoid conflict. The Smithsonian was always going to encounter controversy – from either veteran or peace groups – in the way it displayed the aeroplane. Rather, what this example illustrates is that heritage professionals – and what they do – are an active and integral part of the political process, and that this is unavoidable.

Tunbridge and Ashworth (1996: 122) suggest that perhaps the most obvious illustration of dissonance comes from the heritage of genocide, particularly the Holocaust of the Second World War, which saw the planned and deliberate extermination of millions of people, predominantly of Jewish descent. The museumification of concentration camps such as Auschwitz-Birkenau (Figure 2.1) inevitably evokes debate, emotion and

contestation, as a range of disparate interest groups and stakeholders attempt to negotiate the appropriate handling of such a
painful and extreme past. Some are bound by memories of
abandonment and a 'loss of trust in the world', others by
shame, remorse and responsibility, and others still characterise these reawakened memories as a 'festering wound'
(Wood 1998: 258). Likewise, the notorious history surrounding
the deployment of atomic bombs over Hiroshima and Nagasaki
marks up contentious negotiations between 'victim' and 'perpe-
trator' memorialisation, and contestations over 'responsibility'
and selective remembering of the past within Japan (Siegenthaler 2002: 1122). This is a point illustrated by the contested
narratives surrounding the inscription of the Hiroshima Peace
Memorial onto the World Heritage List, which revolved around
notions of the dome as either a symbol of peace (as ICOMOS
and Japan constructed it) or a symbol of war (as the US Ad-
ministration constructed it in its initial opposition) (Beazley
2007: 34) (see Figure 3.1).

Unlike the *Enola Gay*, the city of Hiroshima and the Hiroshima Peace Memorial Park, which includes the Peace
Memorial Museum and Hiroshima Peace Memorial, or A-bomb
Dome (Genbaku Dome), are already popular tourist attractions
for both domestic and international visitors to Japan. A range
of disparate groups make the 'pilgrimage' to Hiroshima each
year, including ex-combatants, casual tourists, recreation-
seekers and 'grief tourists' (Cooper 2006), where they engage in
difficult, and often contradictory, processes of negotiation between understanding Japan as 'victim', 'aggressor' or both. For
example, Western tourists often see and promote the Hiroshima Peace Memorial as a site for world peace, yet it
simultaneously triggers a range of memories fraught with
pain, horror and suffering for its local, regional and national
communities. As Siegenthaler (2002) notes, both Hiroshima
and Nagasaki thus also operate as sites for 'amnesiac history',
in which an active and deliberate marginalisation of memories
occurs. This is the case not only for America, but also for Japan
as a country coming to terms with what is widely considered 'a

3.1. Hiroshima Peace Memorial Park, including the 'Cenotaph for the A-Bomb Victims' in the foreground, through which the Hiroshima Peace Memorial – or 'A-Bomb Dome' or 'Genbaku Dome' – can be seen. The Hiroshima Peace Memorial was inscribed on UNESCO's World Heritage List in 1996. [Photo: E. Waterton]

crime against humanity', while simultaneously grappling with the silenced memories of Japan's role in the war prior to August 1945 (Cooper 2006: 219). This, as Cooper (2006) among others has argued, creates a complex and contradictory space within which individuals, communities and nations negotiate identity, place and belonging. Cooper goes on to argue that engaging with the Nagasaki Peace Park is likely to have profound emotional consequences for a range of visitors, the majority of whom are seeking to make connections with personal, familial, national and international identities.

This 'dark tourism', or thanatourism, is often characterised as 'heritage' *because of* the lessons it can pass on from the past. This educational underpinning is the one unifying positive to be drawn out of those histories, as it is supposed to engender an awareness that will prevent their recurrence (Ashworth 2002: 364; Simon 2006). Yet, for all our apparent interest in this overarching humanitarian message, it is itself a point of contention. Two related points can be made from this. First, atrocity and genocide are extreme, and it is in this extremity that such events cease to be able to impart applicable and consistent lessons for our everyday lives (Novick 1998: 261). What they can do, however, is effectively mask over and sanitise those everyday legacies of discrimination, racism and uneven power relations that are emphatically *not* atrocity or genocide, and which by comparison, *don't look so bad* (ibid.: 261; Wood 1998). If there *are* lessons to be extracted, as Novick (1998: 261-2) argues, then that encounter with the past:

> ... has to be with the past in all its messiness; they're not likely to come from an encounter with the past that's been shaped and shaded so that inspiring lessons will emerge ... Awe and horror when confronting the Holocaust – for the first time or the thousandth time; then, now, and forever – are surely appropriate. Yet no matter how broadly we interpret the word 'lesson', that's not a lesson – certainly not a useful one.

Second, the official and institutional messages projected as part of the commemoration of atrocity are not necessarily the same as those received by audiences, visitors and users (Ashworth 2002: 364). Thus, while laudable attempts may be made regarding lessons to be learnt, it cannot be assumed that it will be those messages that are taken away, or that they will be inevitably positive and consistent. Rather, this humanitarian agenda is itself a part of the wider process within which heritage professionals encounter and mitigate dissonance, and within which further messages, emotions and responses for various individuals and community groups will be at stake.

This suggestion that lessons can be learnt from dissonant heritage underpins Tunbridge and Ashworth's (1996: 263) optimistic assumption that it can be avoided, or, at the very least, eliminated and/or diffused. Furthermore, Tunbridge and Ashworth intimate that resolving the tensions and conflicts that come with dissonance can be engendered by a turn to 'inclusive' agendas. But what does inclusivity mean in terms of heritage? In England, certainly, it means smoothing out the lines of dissent and exclusion through participation and information, the end result of which sees excluded groups re-educated and in a position to 'better' understand the cultural symbols, tastes and choices of the included, the ruling elite. Building on Richardson's (2007: 35) arguments about hegemony, it becomes possible to see that this sort of responsiveness to dissonance 'in no way disrupts the privilege and dominance of the ruling classes'. Rather, 'dissonant heritage' is simply understood as an alternative, or counterpart, to consensual 'heritage', and then there are '*specific* conflicts or dissonant events that will arise in the management of heritage from time to time' (Smith 2006: 82, emphasis in original). In following this logic, the aim of the management process in England, as Waterton (2007a) has argued, is one that explicitly attempts to disassociate from 'recent' and 'subjective' pasts as a means of mitigating conflict. It is precisely for this reason that the term 'heritage' has been replaced by the term 'historic environment', as while the former means 'very different things to different people', and is thus difficult and contentious, the latter is assumed to be 'a more neutral term' (English Heritage 2000b: 5) or a 'safer term' (cited in Waterton 2007a: 221). Not only is the historic environment considered neutral and safe, it is also considered 'the *best* of our past' (DCMS 2001: 33), and thus something that should impart a positive experience, as the following reveals:

Of course, not all of the historic environment is equally valuable or worth conserving; some of it indeed has a negative impact on all who experience it (English Heritage 2005c: 1).

Dissonant or 'negative' heritage thus becomes something that is undesirable and to be avoided. The mechanism that has arisen in the UK for dealing with this need to eradicate dissonance has come in the form of 'inclusion'. Here, community groups and individuals operating outside dominant understandings of heritage are subsumed, through policy, practice and rhetoric, into dominant understandings, the argument being that dissonance can – and will – be avoided by asserting a consensual heritage. One of the significant consequences of this is not simply that some types or forms of heritage will be marginalised or deemed not to exist, but that it will also have significant consequences for heritage policies and practices of social inclusion. Since the election of Blair's New Labour Government in 1997, social inclusion has been a dominant policy directive within the cultural sector. However, attempts to engender 'inclusion' through mechanisms that smooth out dissent and contention are likely to lead to the cultural or social assimilation of the excluded.

'Heritage' versus 'dissonant heritage'

While we do not agree with the distinction implied between 'heritage' and 'dissonant heritage', we do concede that it is an idea that carries relevance *as an observation*. It is a distinction that extends beyond the pages of Tunbridge and Ashworth's work and is reflected in the heritage policy process, at least in England. As we have documented above, the management process tends to operate around the assumption that there is 'good' heritage and 'negative' heritage, and the latter can be

65

avoided by focussing on the former. For us, this presents something of a paradox: on the one hand, we accept that all heritage is inherently dissonant by virtue of the complexity of society. On the other hand, heritage in the UK is regulated by a discourse that requires *all* notions of heritage that fall *outside* an image of consensual heritage – dissonant heritage – to acquiesce to a dominant discourse. The process thus becomes circular, in which all heritage is continually pressed out, smoothed over and presented as safe, good and consensual. A useful example of this comes from Britain's response to the wider international reawakening of 'moral issues', and global attempts to open up the past as an area of debate (Macdonald 2005: 51). Two recent events characterise this response: the first, national Holocaust Memorial Day, 27 January 2001, and the year-long commemoration of the bicentenary of the abolition of the British slave trade in 2007, both of which are, categorically, areas of extreme dissonance.

The acknowledgement and commemoration of the Holocaust and the trans-Atlantic slave trade in Britain are both difficult. We make this statement not only because both encompass profoundly traumatic and emotional memories, but also because identity, and especially *national* identity, is assumed to be safe, good, heroic and stable within the dominant heritage narrative. This carries significant implications for the range of interest groups engaging in their commemoration, including those heritage and museum professionals involved in the interpretation and presentation of these histories. While there is no real story of triumph to be had from the Holocaust for Britain, unlike commemorations of the slave trade, the wider approach to both was inextricably shot through with issues of dissonance as political and institutional directives sought to assert images of consensus rather than conflict. Indeed, in peeling back the initial veneer of 'national remembering', it quickly became apparent that these events were being used as mechanisms, or 'collective memories', that would promote a particular ideal of Britishness and consensus (ibid.: 60). This was specifically the case for both examples, in which political set-pieces highlighted the need to focus on 'unity' and 'togetherness' rather than examining the needs, memories and disparate requirements of a range of stakeholders and interest groups. Within the context of the bicentenary, Tony Blair, then Prime Minister of the UK, reinforced this message of unity and consensus by declaring, 'this is everyone's bicentenary' (Blair 2007: 1). Rather than emphasising diversity and contention, the commemoration of both the Holocaust and the bicentenary became contexts within which to reassert the ideals of Britishness and gloss over inequities in existing social relations. In making appeals to a far wider collective – the national community – the discursive spaces within which dissonance could be engaged with were closed and replaced by what Wetherell and Potter (1992) refer to as a 'togetherness' motif. This may seem an obvious point, but it is the implications of this call for 'togetherness' that are of interest. By denying the centrality of dissonance to heritage, and not just in relation to the memorialisation of the Holocaust and the abolition of slavery, it becomes difficult for community groups that sit *outside* this repertoire of togetherness, or take issue with the institutional messages imparted, to be heard and their expressions legitimised.

The bicentenary was an event explicitly opposed by a number of community groups within the UK, including the Ligali Organisation (Ligali 2005), Bristol's black community (Gabriel 2007), Operation Truth (2007), communities of African British (Bona Sawa 2007) and the Consortium of Black Groups (COBG) (COBG 2007; for other oppositional accounts, see Gabriel 2007). Toyin Agbetu from Ligali publicly and vocally expressed his dissent and opposition to the 2007 commemorations at the Westminster Abbey service commemorating the anniversary of the abolition (BBC 2007; Ligali 2000-07; Agbetu & Pierre 2008). The commemorative emphasis on the role of named individuals within the abolition process, in particular that of William Wilberforce, and its overarching tendency to cast the role of African people as 'passive recipients of emancipation' (Ligali 2005: 5), were prominent concerns. Likewise, community groups opposed to the celebrations cited a focus on the injustices of the past, and thus an obscuring of current forms of inequality within Britain. As the Consortium of Black Groups (COBG 2007) position statement remarks:

> ... people of Afrikan descent have a right to determine what aspects of this traumatic period of our history should be commemorated and in what way. The fight for freedom and our continued quest for justice in the educational system, housing, employment and mental health and penal institutions, demonstrates that our situation has not changed to any great extent.

Dissonance, here, revolves around a disjuncture between what *is* being remembered and what *ought* to be remembered, and the realisation that 'it is always possible to remember otherwise' (Hesse 2002: 146). While the bicentenary is very much located within a cultural space replete with different terms of remembering, dilemmas of responsibility, and possibilities for genuine recognition of past and present histories, it effectively obscures the struggle of remembering slavery, both within the dominant white population and between different community groups. The form of commemoration taken up by parliament is thus one that 'remembers' something quite different to what other areas of the population might have expected, focussing primarily on the benevolence of Britain in terms of abolition, rather than on the highly-organised, predatory violence of the slave trade itself. The anniversary of abolition embarks on a process of erasure, not only in terms of alternative frames of history, but in how the present identity of Britain is constructed: as unified, moral and shared. As Hesse (2002: 158) has discussed in relation to the remembrance of abolition in the US, this valorisation and prioritisation of a 'multicultural' and 'cosmopolitan' society is nothing new. What it does do, however, is enforce a silence on African British community groups by ignoring alternative or hidden/unspoken histories, particularly in relation to contemporary inequities, governance and forms of cultural representation.

Consensual and comfortable heritage
can be dissonant too

While the case studies examined so far have tended to operate around the extremities of dissonance, we suggest that dissonance will occur every time we engage with heritage. It is not possible to smooth out dissent, as heritage is about the negotiation of cultural meaning and it is vary rare in any society for there to be universal acceptance of any given value or cultural narrative – even consensual history is not universal, as consensus itself implies some level of dissent and compromise. Yet, if we think of heritage simply as a site, building or artefact, then dissonance and conflict become more manageable as they become contained by the boundaries of the site or the physical limits of the building. Thus the wider networks of social and cultural debate within which they may sit are easier to ignore. It is also easy to ignore dissonance when a site or place sits within consensual or dominant narratives of history. The English country house, or stately home, is the epitome of national heritage in England. Not only are these sites hailed as some of the finest examples of Britain's architectural and cultural heritage, they represent a multi-million pound industry.

Valued within the AHD for their aesthetic and architectural values, these sites are portrayed, often entirely unproblematically, as sites or places representative of *national* history. Indeed, Margaret Hodge, Minister of State for Culture, Media and Sport, recently remarked that citizenship ceremonies for new British citizens should be undertaken in such historic houses, castles and other similar heritage places so that people could 'associate their new citizenship with key cultural icons' (2008). However, country houses and other iconic historic buildings are not always seen as such. For instance, visitors to labour heritage museums, when asked to define heritage, noted:

Stately homes is a dominant idea [of heritage], but for me it is the whole history – more than just kings and queens

69

and politicians. The traditional view of heritage represents only the top level of society. ... this [the labour
history museum] is the other side of history than was
taught at schools or traditionally seen as heritage. The
nineteenth century as taught in schools in my day was
about Empire and how great Great Britain was – this is
the other side of that history (quoted in Smith 2006: 211).

Or, more cynically:

[heritage is] working class history as opposed to seeing a
stately home where the landed gentry live [said sneer-
ingly], country houses are interesting in themselves but
there is only so much you can learn from them, and why
would I pay someone to look around their house – they
can pay me 10 quid to look around mine (quoted in Smith
2006: 212).

As these remarks illustrate, country houses can be dissonant,
too. In the quotations above, they are seen as dissonant because of what they stand for. They are identified as the authorised symbol of heritage, the icons that Hodge identified, but
rather than celebrated as Hodge would suggest, they are seen
as working to deny the legitimacy of other forms of heritage, in
this case working-class history and heritage. They can also
mask and deny other forms of heritage and history; here a
visitor to a country house notes that they are:

Comfortable about visiting [the country house] even
though it was built on slavery, but nonetheless it's part of
the country's history (country house visitor, quoted in
Smith 2006: 141).

The history of enslavement is acknowledged, but dismissed as
central or significant to the country's history. This dismissal is
more actively done by the following visitor to a country house
during 2007 when asked if they had come to see the exhibition

the house was putting on to mark the bicentenary of Britain's abolition of its slave trade:

> No, not really, it is irrelevant, we came to see the house, the history of princess Mary, the royal family, so it's a [...] kind of separate issue to visit here, so we kind of passed it by.[3]

The visitor does not see the relevance of the exhibition, as for them the house and its history are about royalty. The fact that the house in question was built on the back of the slave trade simply does not register, and it is 'passed by'. In this case, dissonance may be seen in the way the country house – and the meanings it has for visitors and British society at large – denies the relevance of African British history. Although the country house is nationally valued and recognised as some-thing beautiful, comfortable, grand and 'good', this is in itself dissonant. It is dissonant as this comfortable construction of heritage works to deny or gloss over the brutalities of class, ethnic and cultural inequalities that supported the lifestyles of the rural elites.

Similarly, work by both Jones (2004) and Waterton (2005) has examined some of the conflicts that can occur within the management of legitimised 'objects' of heritage – in these cases, a Pictish cross-slab and an area of national park. In both examples, nationally recognised instances of 'heritage' have become imbued with conflict and controversy surrounding their management and control. These disputes are not the stuff of atrocity, nor are they stuff of active political marginalisation. What they are, however, are examples of resistance from *within* the dominant majority *against* consensual, and quite often banal, narratives of heritage. There is nothing particu-larly problematic about early medieval sculpture or the situating of a community within the boundaries of a national park within the AHD. Both quite comfortably fall within the parameters of authenticity and significance asserted by the AHD, and as such, *should* tell us something about the consen-sual nature of heritage. That these examples are still oppositional in some way, and provide a source of conflict, tells us something rather different about the nature of heritage, and what it tells us is that there will *always* be elements of dissent.

Jones (2004), in her examination of the personal and emotional conflicts surrounding the Hilton of Cadboll, notes that for heritage professionals notions of ownership are often seen as something of an irrelevance. For the local community, however, the cross-slab is conceived of as a member of their community, with 'rights', 'charisma', 'feelings' and a 'soul' (Jones 2004: 50). With the excavation of the lower portion of the cross-slab in 2001, the community of Hilton of Cadboll entered into a long-lasting and acrimonious engagement with a range of national heritage bodies and various communities of professionals over its 'repatriation' (Jones 2006: 107). In line with national policy, which grants authority to heritage professionals in terms of conservation, the inevitable course of action proposed was to remove the lower portion of the cross-slab for both immediate and long-term conservation needs. This was greeted with a significant volume of local resistance seeking to challenge the focus on 'historical significance' and 'historic fabric' espoused by heritage organisations, particularly Historic Scotland, and professionals involved in the conflict (Jones 2004: 52). For the local residents, the cross-slab was conceived of as a living thing, complete with complex social and symbolic dimensions, and, importantly, with a concrete and *real* place within the community (Jones 2006: 117). In challenging the dominant assumptions of heritage values, the people of Hilton of Cadboll, and specifically the Hilton Historic Trust, found themselves ensnared in a debate between another community of interest whose professional identities were tied up in precisely the discourse they were seeking to denounce.

The wider community of Hilton were also embroiled in negotiations within the local community between perceived 'insiders' and 'outsiders' (Jones 2004: 53). As Jones points out, the Hilton Historic Trust developed to accommodate the interests of the villages, and, as it is predominantly made up of 'insiders', was seen within the community as that most closely associated with the residents of Hilton. This clustering of groups *within* the local community itself became a source of confusion and contestation, which can perhaps be seen as a symptom of the uncritical idea of 'community' embedded in policy. Rather than assume that residents of Hilton held a heterogeneous and at times conflicting range of views, the heritage professionals involved had a tendency to communicate with only one of the established community groups, rather than with them all. Thus struggles for authority and control, and wider instances of dissonance, were negotiated not only in and between the wider community of Hilton and heritage professionals, but within that community itself, a point often overlooked within heritage policy and practice.

Likewise, the Bellingham community in Northumberland views the Hareshaw Linn, which is situated within the boundaries of the Northumberland National Park, as a very personal and 'magic' place, replete with memories and a deep sense of place that permeates the local community (Waterton 2005). The management policy for the National Park, however, does not recognise the Linn in terms of its cultural and contemporary values, focussing instead on compartmentalising the natural from the cultural, and the past from the present. The Hareshaw Linn Project, which emerged from a Village Appraisal in 1996 and formally began in 1999, was an attempt to steer the focus on the National Park towards recognition of the social and cultural values invested in the Linn by the local community. The project was steered by the Hareshaw Linn Local Community Group, which comprised representatives from the Parish Council, District Council, Rural Community Council and the Bellingham Community Council, and worked in association with staff from the National Park Authority (Northumberland National Park 1999). From the outset, the project was greeted with collective resistance, bound up not only with the usual complex internal relationships of community groups, but with external relationships with the National Park that were built upon a history of mistrust. The range of projects and events that took place under the umbrella of the

Hareshaw Linn Project included a variety of people from the Bellingham community, including Bellingham First School, Bellingham Community Middle School, the Youth Group, the Bellingham Beavers and Brownies groups, local writing, drama and art classes, the Natural History Society and a range of individuals involved in interpretive projects.

Within the complex process of working through the Hareshaw Linn Project, many people within the village of Bellingham sought to imagine a role for the Linn that stood in opposition to dominant understandings of landscape. This is not to say that the Hareshaw Linn experience is an example of contentious or difficult histories, but rather, that it *became* contentious and difficult because of the conflicting social messages and purposes that that history was imagined to fulfil and inform. Nor was the management plan proposed by the Northumberland National Park an active attempt to marginalise the community of Bellingham, rather it was a more or less straightforward attempt by a larger institutional body to 'manage' and interpret heritage within the confines of the dominant discourse. As with the Hilton of Cadboll example, ownership of the Linn was a significant source of conflict that extended from its purchase by the National Park Authority in 1974 (Thompson & Thompson 1999). As a consequence, the National Park Authority was not only attempting to manage what they perceived as an archaeological and historical resource, but a complex process of disassociation and disempowerment felt by the local community in response to that loss of legal ownership. Acknowledging this sense of lost ownership was a particularly powerful facet of the community projects instigated by the people of Bellingham, and was a significant recommendation emerging from the Hareshaw Oral History Community Project (Mitchell 1999). The Hilton of Cadboll and the Hareshaw Linn offer potent examples of the tensions that emerge when a community group is not granted the space within which to negotiate, assert and reconsider what heritage *means* to it.

Conclusion: all heritage is dissonant

If heritage is multi-faceted and ultimately experienced in the present, then dissonance becomes unavoidable. The momentum offered by dissonance lies not with its associations with difficult or uncomfortable heritages, although it is perhaps easier to 'see' it in these contexts, but as something that is part of all heritage encounters. There are two points worth stressing here. The first draws from Pearson and Sullivan's (1995) idea that the role of heritage managers is to mitigate conflict over heritage when it occurs. Pearson and Sullivan (1995) are talking, in large part, about the mitigation of conflicts over land use, often between developers and heritage managers. Certainly, many heritage managers consider that one of their main responsibilities is ensuring the protection, conservation or salvage of archaeological and/or heritage material in the face of land use conflicts. However, heritage management is also about *social* conflict. Heritage, and those professionals who mange, curate, interpret and research those things that communities define as heritage, are implicated in the governance and arbitration of consensual social and cultural narratives and the recognition or misrecognition of community identities and histories. Heritage management is not simply about the technical issues surrounding the assessment and mitigation of environmental impacts, nor is research undertaken, discussed or disseminated in a social and cultural vacuum. How heritage is, or is not, managed impacts upon community and wider social debates and narratives about the meaning of the past for the present. The narratives that heritage professionals construct have a social effect on political and cultural debates. Communities in various different forms and ways engage with, reject, negotiate or assimilate those narratives and stories. They also use them in a variety of ways to support their own agendas. Thus, often unwittingly, heritage professionals become engaged in the mitigation of social and political conflict and dissonance. Rather than reject or run from this, heritage professionals need to develop an active sense of their role in 'mitigating' social conflict and understanding the social, political and cultural dimensions and consequences of this, so that they may take an active and informed stance within the processes of social arbitration.

The second point is that not all conflict can or should be mitigated. Heritage is *about* working through conflicts. It is a process in flux as populations and communities negotiate and revaluate the cultural and social values that they think are – or are not – important. The past, like memory, is inevitably reworked and given new meanings and narratives as various communities, including communities of expertise, assert and attempt to fulfil their particular agendas. The values and meanings we give to heritage change – not only over time but between and within communities. This variation and diversity is natural and healthy. If we can see heritage as a process of working *with* this diversity, and see it as a process through which we define those values from both the past and present that societies and communities wish to 'preserve' and pass on, then conflict need not necessarily be negative. This is because community conflict and dissonance with authorised heritage narratives provides an opportunity for communities *as well as* experts to reconsider the legitimacy and utility of historical and cultural narratives and agendas. Understanding the dissonant nature of heritage, together with understanding the social consequences that heritage can have for communities, requires us to appreciate the effectiveness of debate. Informed debate between communities and the communities of experts can be a useful and informative process for all concerned. However, real debate also requires an understanding of the position of power that professionals tend to occupy relative to many other communities within the heritage management process. Rather than assuming a position of 'top down' expertise, engagement with community dissonance requires a reconsideration of the way experts engage in the mitigation and arbitration of conflicts – not only will it be impossible to solve all conflicts, experts do not always have to 'win'.

4

Having a stake

Introduction

In taking notions of power, culture and identity seriously, we have inevitably stumbled upon a more explicitly political topic than the title of this volume might initially suggest: the politics of recognition. In many ways this topic is symptomatic of the times, as it is concerned with a type of social justice claim that resonates with wider contemporary debates concerned with multiculturalism and minority rights on the one hand, and civic engagement and deliberative democracy on the other. The concepts of status and self-image, both of which are sometimes greeted with political unease because of perceived threats they are assumed to make against aspirations for social cohesion and consensus, are key to the politics of recognition (Philips 1995: 22). One of the central arguments that we have so far advanced revolves around this idea of 'consensus', which we have problematised because of the consequences it has for community groups seeking to assert an alternative under-standing of heritage. Indeed, the net result of this fixation with consensus has been the virtual disappearance of dissonance and more nuanced ways of understanding heritage. Tied to this argument has been our underlying assurance that 'identity' – and here we mean multiple and competing identities – is not something we should be afraid of. Rather it is something that is neither good nor bad, as it is simply mobilised, reinforced, challenged, amended, negated, played out and/or created every time we engage with and experience heritage. As such, quite how identity is tied up in our experiences of heritage, and how it becomes something that is often put at stake

within the management process, needs to be both acknowledged and understood.

The idiom of recognition inevitably plays a role in any community heritage project on some level, whether in terms of the
more obvious political agendas self-consciously invoked in
struggles in post-colonial nations, as part of more banal attempts by local groups to lead in the interpretation of their past
at community, regional and national levels, or *within* groups as
they negotiate issues of value and meaning. This chapter illustrates this union between heritage and recognition. Our aim is
not simply to document this relationship but make clear the
thornier implications this has for notions of expertise and ideas
of 'community'. Through the theoretical lens offered by the
'politics of recognition', current practices will be reframed and
revised, and the hitherto largely ignored areas of community
identity, self-worth and control will be examined.

What is at stake? The politics of recognition
and identity politics

The words 'identity politics' are all too often used to dismiss
community access to, or interpretations of, heritage. Curiously,
the phrase is seldom used to describe conflicts between heritage professionals and communities when those communities
are deemed to be culturally 'like' those from which the majority
of heritage professionals derive. Identity politics, it would
seem, is an issue we need only confront when dealing with
Indigenous communities in post-colonial contexts, or when the
'otherness' of a community is pronounced. To the contrary, it is
our contention that identity politics play a key role in understanding the tensions that exist between heritage professionals
and communities of interest. For a more sophisticated understanding of what is at stake in conflicts over identity, we turn
to what Fraser (2000) has labelled the 'politics of recognition'.

As Kymlicka and Norman (2000: 3) point out, the notion of
'recognition' emerged from the late twentieth century onwards
and is characterised by a number of political events. These

include the collapse of communism and spread of ethnic nationalism, a backlash against immigration and asylum seekers, the
political mobilisation of Indigenous peoples, and threats of
secession from Quebec, Scotland and Flanders (Ibid; Englund
2004: 1). Within this context, different community groups
made claims for recognition, including both symbolic and material gestures of recognition, along with their anticipated
consequences for respect, identity, self-worth, legal standing,
participation and access to a range of resources (Kymlicka &
Norman 2006: 29).What these groups were reacting to, primarily, was a denial of parity within interactions and decision-
making. While these examples have not always been positive,
as Nancy Fraser (2000) points out, and have in some instances
been tied up with campaigns for ethnic cleansing and genocide,
it is a model that nonetheless has lessons for the realm of
heritage when handled carefully. In the framework devised by
Fraser, the politics of recognition becomes a genuine, emanci-
patory model that is wrapped around a distinct idea of justice,
capable of supporting defensible claims for both equality *and* a
recognition of difference (Fraser 2001: 22). It is based on social
status rather than collective identity, and sees recognition as
something intimately tied up with issues of justice and morality, which collectively provide the conditions for a 'parity of
participation' (ibid.: 29).

While the phrase itself is more commonly associated with
explicitly political agendas seeking to address oppression in the
form of misrecognition or lack of recognition, it is not the
prerogative of particular countries or specific groups of people
(Englund 2004: 3). It also has implications – not of all of which
are comfortable in terms of current heritage practices – for
ongoing negotiations within the context of community heri-
tage/archaeology projects, particularly in terms of the break
Fraser makes with notions of 'identity' and identity politics
(ibid.: 24). Fraser argues that this break is necessary as to do
otherwise runs the risk of *denying* the complexity of social
groups (and indeed the relations of power existing within
them), and imposing an essentialised group identity (ibid.: 24).

79

In other words, if recognition were to revolve around group identity, enormous amounts of pressure would be placed upon group members to conform to that simplified group identity (ibid.: 24). For this reason, Fraser offers something she refers to as 'the status model' of recognition, which does not privilege collective identity as such, but rather the *status* of group members 'as full partners in social interaction' (ibid.: 24). This allows us to examine the heritage management process in terms of status equality and reciprocal recognition on the one hand, and misrecognition and status subordination on the other (Fraser 2000: 113). In particular, it allows us to specifically examine avenues of community involvement, the parameters of which we have thus far argued impede parity of participation for a range of communities because of the narrow collection of cultural norms and symbols embedded within heritage institutions, policy and practice. Fraser's model of recognition provides a framework from which to explore what exactly is at stake when communities are denied the opportunity to interact as full partners *on a par* with communities of expertise, and, perhaps to a lesser degree, communities that conform to the idea of heritage that currently animates policy and practice. This denial, as Fraser (1999: 35, emphasis in original) argues, is 'a consequence of *institutionalised* patterns of cultural value that constitute one as comparatively unworthy of respect or esteem'. In terms of heritage and archaeology, this has meant that communities of expertise have been placed in a position to regulate and assess the relative *worth* of other communities of interest, both in terms of their aspirations and identities. Moreover, this notion of 'worth' is more often than not tied up with a white middle-class sense of heritage. 'Other' communities, therefore, have endured a less than equal footing from which to make claims about their past, their heritage and their self-image.

The case studies in this chapter give insight into what is at stake for community groups as a consequence of this lack of parity. We are not suggesting that a particular community group *should* be prioritised, nor should communities of expertise be ignored and downplayed. What we *are* suggesting, however, is that each engagement with heritage requires a diligent approach that is conscious of the possibility for misrecognition and actively attempts to provide parameters for equitable interactions. These interactions must also take account of the historical and contemporary contexts of engagement, so that traditional positions of privilege are acknowledged and amended. This is certainly not a model that seeks to say that *every* claim for recognition is valid, nor one that advocates the exacerbation of difference. Rather, the opening up of conceptual spaces within which cross-group interactions – and here we mean interactions across and within communities of heritage, including those of expertise – can take place equitably, within fair conditions and equal opportunities (Fraser 1999: 35). This is not to suggest that wider inequitable relationships, terms of injustice and access to resources will not also impede parity of participation outside the immediate realm of heritage, but this is not our focus here. Instead, this chapter draws on Fraser's conceptualisation of 'recognition' to argue for a heritage practice that identifies subordinate status within the management process and reconstitutes those groups so that they find an equitable position from which to interact *fully, as peers* (Fraser 2001: 27) within heritage engagements and experiences.

Indigenous heritage and claims for recognition

An obvious place to begin to examine the issues at stake is within the context of post-colonial countries, where claims for recognition are more easily discerned. Particularly vociferous Indigenous reactions have emerged in response to the excavation, collection, interpretation and display of their cultural and ancestral remains (Atalay 2006: 288). Not only do these reactions reveal a nuanced account of what communities *do* when they engage with heritage, in terms of their desires and aspirations, they also offer insight into what is at *stake*. If we take

Australia as a starting point, we can see that these claims for recognition take place within a context that is deeply colonial and characterised by acts of violence, dispossession, appropriation, marginalisation and racism (McNiven & Russell 2005). This colonial legacy constrains conditions for equitable participation in a range of ways. For a start, considerable power is lent to archaeological knowledge, expertise and 'white'/'European' modes of 'knowing' the past, in contrast to the limited legitimacy extended to Indigenous ways of knowing and understanding their history. In addition, the very notion of Aboriginal Australians, as Smith and Jackson (2006) point out, is couched in terms of cultural stasis, which is rendered legitimate only through appeals to tradition and continuity, and inevitably requires 'proof' or verification from communities of expertise. Moreover, the notion of 'Aboriginal' is also imagined in the singular, with a striking homogeneity implied, so as to collapse the distinctions, complexities and diversities that exist in and among Aboriginal communities across Australia (Smith & Jackson 2006). In response, Australian Indigenous people have contested the use of the old colonial descriptors of 'Aborigine' and 'Aboriginal' and have asserted a new and complex layering of identity to recognise not only the diversity of their identities, but also the similarities of their political experiences and aspirations. As James Miller notes 'the term Aboriginal did not give my people a separate identity' (1986: vii), and while specific community names give local identity, regional identities are also proclaimed by the use of names such as Koori, Murri, Nunga, Pallawa, and Nyoongar among others. These latter terms not only recognise regional Australian Indigenous cultural identities and ties, but also implicitly recognise the collective identities and communities forged through the experiences of racism and dispossession that commenced with the colonial invasion of Australia. Internationally, the use of the collective term Indigenous – spelt self-consciously with a capital 'I' – asserts and requires recognition of a collective political identity and community. Indigenous not only refers to the dictionary definition of someone native to a particular place

(and in this case specifically colonised places), but, more importantly, asserts a collective identity based on the continuing
experiences of colonial and post-colonial disenfranchisement
and continuing struggles for self-determination and sover-
eignty. Thus Indigenous peoples are not simply 'indigenous',
but are proclaiming their shared and disparate identities as
people involved in local, national and international struggles
for respect, human rights and resources.

Although claims for Indigenous recognition are often formed
around land-rights claims, reburial issues and debates about
repatriation, so much more is actually at stake. Indeed, such
claims are also often responses to threats to self-image, identity
formation, cultural rights and control over senses of self, community and heritage, as Ros Langford so eloquently and powerfully
argued in her 1983 paper, *Our Heritage – Your Playground*. As an
awareness of this history and its consequences for archaeologi-
cal/heritage practice continues to grow, a range of heritage
professionals, academics, Indigenous communities, non-Indigenous communities and pockets of wider society find themselves
in a situation where they must re-define and re-manage their
relationships with each other (Smith & Jackson 2006: 312).

Heidi Ellemor (2003), for example, has examined the politics
of belonging within the Barmah-Millewa Forest, south-eastern
Australia, in relation to both the Yorta Yorta community and
local, non-Indigenous community groups. Her analysis revolves
around notions of 'sense of place', or 'politics of place', and
examines how communities of expertise – through the *Native
Title Act* – are used to mediate the experiences and constructions of place created by competing community groups. This
prospect for mediation came as a consequence of the lodging of
a Native Title Claim by the Yorta Yorta community in 1994,
which sought to have rights and responsibilities to traditional
lands and water, along with associated customs, practices,
stories and traditions, recognised – an aim that was contested
by many parties (Ellemor 2003: 239). The original judgement
in December 1998 gave a negative ruling, which was upheld on
appeal in 2001 by the Federal Court and again in 2002 by the

High Court of Australia (Sculthorpe 2005: 179). What is at the heart of this example is the issue of control, not only in terms of access and ownership but over the past itself, in which two oppositional versions of history and their attendant contemporary identities seek to be heard and acknowledged (Ellemor 2003: 237). For the Yorta Yorta, this sense of self-image and heritage arises out of the transmission of memories through family, a feeling of connection and attachment with place, and a sense of belonging to the area. While it may appear to be a simple claim for traditional land and water, it is also tied up with ideas of kinship/family, remembrance, special places, stories and daily life, all intricately interwoven and embodied within and across that landscape.

As Ellemor points out, the negative Yorta Yorta decision was in many ways a response to the 'Aboriginalisation' of non-Indigenous connections to the forest, which simultaneously de-Aboriginalised Indigenous attempts to satisfy criteria of distinctiveness and continuity. In order to contest the Yorta Yorta claims for Native Title, local, non-Indigenous community groups destabilised the status of those participating in the Claim by invoking a similar language of attachment, emotion and social history. While this may at first appear an act based on the promotion of parity, in reality it rests on a wider failure to take account of the traditional position of Aboriginal people as *subordinate* actors within the heritage process. The Yorta Yorta decision was based upon disparities in participation borne out of the institutionalised understanding of an Aboriginal 'community', in which the demonstration of continuance required by Native Title was judged using criteria of 'tradition' and 'authenticity' – verified by anthropological and archaeological expertise – that in effect declared the contemporary identities of that particular community to be inauthentic (ibid.: 241).

This example is useful for illustrating the problematics of identity politics for issues of recognition, as the possibilities for change, diversity and internal heterogeneity were denied in favour of a search for an 'authentic' and drastically simplified group identity. Little allowance was made for the historical, political and cultural contexts within which such claims operate, nor, as Porter (2004) remarks, were those groups that stood in opposition to Indigenous claims asked to 'unlearn' their privileges – in terms of archaeological knowledge and 'white' history. Similar examples from the Australian context can also be drawn upon to shed light on the complex issue of recognition, particularly in terms of misrecognition and injustice as a consequence of conventional archaeological and heritage practices, and the subsequent status subordination of Indigenous people (Smith & Wobst 2005; Clarke & Faulker 2005; Porter 2006).

The Indigenous cultures of Mexico, as Nalda (2005: 33) observes, have a long history of being characterised as people with no history, or, at least, no part to play in what has been traditionally revered as the 'glorious past' of Mexico, resulting in a systematic rejection of contemporary Indigenous cultures. Even as the pasts of Indigenous groups gained visibility in the tourism market, those associated communities remained economically and politically marginalised (Hoobler 2006: 447). As such, it is unsurprising that Mexico has a more recent history punctuated by political struggles for recognition that have resonance for economic, social and cultural spheres in the form of revenue, respect and genuine incorporation of Indigenous perspectives into narratives of national history (Vanden Berghe & Maddens 2004). A principal way in which this quest for recognition has played out in Oaxaca, as Hoobler (2006) documents, is through Indigenous self-representation in community museums. What was at stake in this example is easy to see, as the area's history is inextricably tied up with marginalisation. Involvement in a range of community museum projects provided an opportunity to assume a semblance of control over the past and a means to affirm and legitimise both past and contemporary self-image. Despite active involvement from two anthropologists in the initial stages of the wider community museums project, it is the communities themselves who are in a position to define and represent their own sense of history and heritage. As one participant from the community of San Miguel del Progreso notes, ownership of the community museums process offered a transformative and emotive experience, in which feelings of shame were replaced with a sense of control and pride (cited in Hoobler 2006: 444). In this particular instance, the subverting of institutionalised patterns of cultural value had a positive, internal effect on individual members of the community group. At stake, then, were not only the broader Indigenous narratives of Mexican history, but individual ideas of self-worth and self-identity also affected by the denial of participatory parity.

A similar case can be considered from Europe as Falch and Skandfer (2004: 361) document in their analysis of Sámi in Norway, and their active use and assertion of local knowledge and cultural heritage as 'a reference point' in their struggles for cultural survival and acknowledgement. As with the case studies above, control over heritage is vital for self-representation, self-determination, cultural continuity and pride. The foundation of Sámi Parliaments in Finland, Norway and Sweden was an event through which those 'of Sámi heritage' were granted a position from which to manage heritage, provide a means of cultural autonomy and attempt to define what it means to be Sámi (Beach 2007). This movement towards the legal recognition of Sámi has not always been easy and continues to be in dispute as each Parliament attempts to navigate others' images of 'Sámi' (often drawn up around genetics, 'blood' and strict linguistic criteria) in relation to their own conceptions of self (Müller & Pettersson 2001; Beach 2007: 16). Moreover, community control does not necessarily equate with recognition. For instance, the Directorate for Cultural Heritage, the Norwegian State agency with overall responsibility for Norwegian heritage, tends to view rock art, a significant aspect of Sámi heritage, as universally significant (Falch and Skandfer 2004). This characterisation relegates Sámi past as peripheral within the Norwegian state, while simultaneously aspects of that past are appropriated into universalising and national narratives. The consequences of this is that 'Sámi are being alienated from their own history', and their history and cultural heritage becomes 'neutralised as a tool in a serious battle for culture and resources' (ibid.: 372). The practices of heritage management all too often misrecognise conflicts over heritage as both case specific and as centring on or resolvable through technical issues of management. This process, as Smith (2004a) has argued, often works to depoliticise the wider politics of identity and recognition. Further, the appropriation of Sámi knowledge and history by a naturalised and nationalising Norwegian narrative about prehistory is an all too recognisable process in the development of archaeological narratives and heritage management, as both are processes predicated upon an ideology of 'universal' value and universal human history. While the ideal of a shared human history is philosophically laudable in one sense, its naïve and wholesale application can disenfranchise or otherwise marginalise the experiences of particular communities or groups, experiences that may need acknowledgment as part of political struggles for recognition and social justice.

Lessons from a decolonising practice

As Atalay (2007: 250) points out, the lessons that we take away from engagements with Indigenous communities in post-colonial countries are useful for collaborative and community experiences in non-Indigenous contexts too. A popularly cited example of a non-Indigenous community archaeology project is the ongoing fieldwork at Catalhöyük, central Turkey, an internationally renowned site some 9,000 years old (see also Hodder 1996). However, Atalay (2007) has examined this case study in terms of what she sees as a lack of substantial local involvement. As well as acknowledging her privilege as both an American and an archaeologist involved on the site, Atalay (2007: 252) also foregrounds the need to engage in a socially-responsible and socially-just practice that takes account of the needs and desires of a range of contemporary communities. These communities include local people living in villages in the region, local people who undertake seasonal work on the site, tourists to the area, New Age Goddess followers, politicians and archaeologists. For example, local communities have been involved through the setting up of a community exhibit in the Visitor Centre on site (from the perspective of local women) and have taken part in post-excavation studies (Hodder 2002: 176). Local voices are thus combined with those of excavators and various specialists in a range of publications and interpretations (Hodder: 2003: 62).

The aim is to move towards forming a collaboratively based encounter with the site that has positive effects for contemporary communities (Atalay 2007: 253). The specifics of this engagement, however, are defined not by attempts to gain control of the excavation and interpretation processes, but to harness the project to wider initiatives that address the need for economic improvement for the area. Recognition, in this sense, does not revolve around a need to have an alternative sense of the past acknowledged, although these communities do care deeply about the site (ibid.: 263), but rather it is about having the right to share in the material benefits associated with it. This is not to say that other stakeholders have not engaged in contested debate around issues of power and status. Indeed, the site is also famous for its association with clay 'Mother Goddess' figurines, and it is with this aspect of its history that a New Age 'Goddess' movement has aligned itself (Meskell 2005). The types of conflict and discord emerging from this intersection of established archaeological voice with dissenting groups at Catalhöyük are not dissimilar to those documented by Barbara Bender (1998) at Stonehenge in association with New Age groups. Here, as with Stonehenge, a range of groups struggle to gain access to an internationally renowned site and have their – often competing – interpretations recognised and legitimised (Meskell 2005: 163). In the context of Catalhöyük, some commentators question the rhetoric of multi-vocality espoused by Ian Hodder, suggesting that the naturalisation of archaeological knowledge as the interpretive authority on all matters archaeological is already invested with too much power for alternative voices to gain parity (Rountree 2007: 14). This line of argument, as Rountree points out, can be observed in the hanging of both the local community women and the Goddess perspective displays on temporary, moveable panels, while the archaeological community's interpretations remain fixed to surrounding walls, implying certainty, authority and stability. For Rountree (2007: 20), this is suggestive of a politics of 'gesture', rather than that of recognition, and thus what is at stake is the recognition of alternative understandings and uses of the past *by* institutionalised bodies of knowledge. The point is that despite a framing of the Catalhöyük site within the terms of multi-vocality, alternative perspectives – be they those of local women or those within the Goddess movement – do not carry the same or equal status as archaeologists, who are granted a greater power to speak for, and about, the site and its interpretations. Consequently, these disparate groups continue to talk past one another in what Rountree (2007: 23) describes as 'parallel monologues to audiences who share their own views of the past'. The sacred pilgrimage to Catalhöyük, fuelled by a desire for inspiration, learning and celebration (Rountree 2007: 23), seems incommensurate with the type of learning tied up with conventional acts of excavating and interpreting the site. In addition, it is also sometimes incommensurate with its valuing of women, which can be problematic for traditional Islamic attitudes towards women still prevalent in contemporary Turkish society (Meskell 2005). The Catalhöyük case study presents a complex situation in which multiple claims for recognition compete, some of which may serve to exacerbate female insubordination and status misrecognition.

Collective memory, identity and belonging in Yorkshire

The Cawood Castle Garth Group (CCGG), a self-identified community heritage group from the village of Cawood, North Yorkshire, is situated within the context of wider calls for 'social inclusion' – an enduring theme of the New Labour government. While this discourse of inclusion has triggered a rhetoric of 'community' value, very little space is designated for genuine participation and collaboration within the management proc-ess in reality (Waterton et al. 2006). Indeed, active agency by non-experts is downplayed, with participation reduced and re-imagined in the form of education and information. One way to understand this union between the AHD and social inclusion is to think of it in terms of Annette Weiner's (1992) 'inalienable possessions' and the practice of 'keeping-while-giving'. Here, heritage has come to be something of an inalienable possession. That is, heritage, at least in England, retains a unique identity as a site, monument or building, and is reified as something that holds an unchanging and innate cultural value. This ren-dering simultaneously confers a particular status upon those people assumed to be in a position to define and unlock that cultural value and educate others about its worth. In this context, heritage has become *symbolically* dense; so dense that, as Weiner (1994: 394) argues, 'others have difficulty prying these treasures away from their owners', or, in terms of management, away from those who find themselves defined as 'caretakers' of the past for future generations. Moreover, as Weiner (1992: 10) points out, 'the person or group that controls [and thus defines] the movement and meaning of such objects inherits an authority and a power over others'. Thus, in a strategy of keeping-while-giving, heritage institutions are able to make rhetorical claims about social inclusion and community cohesion, in which talk of participation, involvement, education and consultation abounds, without ever putting in jeopardy their rights of access and control as cultural experts and custodians.

Community-based heritage in Cawood, North Yorkshire

This line of argument underpins our discussion of Cawood and the CCGG, itself a community within a community, and re-volves around the management of Cawood Castle and Castle

Garth, a partially destroyed castle precinct consisting of a gatehouse, banqueting hall and associated medieval enclosure. These surviving features lie within the boundaries of a Conservation Area and are housed under National Monument number 20539, entitled *Cawood Castle and Castle Garth: Residence of the Archbishop's of York and Associated Enclosure Containing Gardens, Five Fishponds and a Quarry Pit.* Both gatehouse and banqueting hall are Grade I Listed and referenced with Listed Building reference numbers 325885 and 325886 respectively. Of particular interest to the CCGG is the associated trapezoidal enclosure to the south of the two remaining buildings, which offers 4.5 hectares of open space at the centre of the village, typically used for informal recreation activities such as walking, relaxing, and picnicking.

Individuals and groups within Cawood became increasing vocal about the ways in which the Garth was managed, particularly in terms of the limited opportunity this allowed local residents to participate in equitable decision-making processes and foster a sense of ownership and control (Waterton 2007b, 2008b). These reactions against traditional management practices are illustrative not only of potential conflicts within the management process, but also of the competing ways in which heritage may be understood and used to guide a self-conscious dialogue between personal and collective memories, identities and values within a community.

Concepts of belonging, place, community spirit and ownership are embedded within the Garth, which provides links between individuals and groups, past and present, and helps position residents within a geographical community. Borrowing from Crang (1996), each visit to the Garth becomes part of a wider self-reflexive activity, in which complex bundles of enjoyment, knowledge and identity are created, with the Garth acting as a site for performing identities. Indeed, it is a crucial operative within a cultural process of 'elective belonging' (Savage et al. 2005: 29), in which people, both individually and as a group, ascertain feelings of spatial attachment and identity.

This localised discourse stands at odds with the scheduling

process and associated management regimes in Cawood. Central is the idea of ownership. In the 1980s the village collectively accepted an increase in Council Tax so as to purchase the Garth, which at the time was under threat from housing development plans. Despite legal ownership since that time, the village has been given little by way of control to decide the uses, access and interpretation of the Garth. A central aim of the CCGG was to challenge this limited scope for participation and argue that their encounters with the Garth – whether walking across it, talking about it, taking stock of surroundings in it, or thinking about being 'in place' – were as much to do with knowing, caring for and understanding heritage as the dictates of the management process:

> When I look out of my window [at the Garth] and see a sunset or the new fall of snow, I rush out with my camera to capture it ... I will always be grateful to the Parish Council for saving this 'green heart' of the village. (CCF 13[1])

> [The Garth] is the green heart of the community – it is a quiet, peaceful place to walk: alone, with dogs or with children. (CCF 1)

> [The Garth] keeps us rooted in the country and develops a sense of community ... it is a wonderful place for us to visit. (CCF 4)

> I like to sit out in the Garth at night and watch the stars. From there I can see the bright haze over York. I like to sit out there and simply think. (CCF 12)

> The Garth is part of our heritage and culture and it is important that those who care for it look after it. (CCF 1)

We are not suggesting that these attachments to the Garth emerged as a consequence of the housing development threats. Rather, these threats triggered or prompted an awareness of how individuals already responded to the Garth – how they felt, how they moved, how they remembered – in a process that was not always easy. They were committed to the integrity of the Garth, but not always in a way that was recognisable in a policy sense. Institutionalised understandings of public, cultural and community value paradoxically worked to disadvantage people in Cawood, preventing them from actively and meaningfully engaging with what they saw as their heritage. The CCGG mobilised against this lack of parity and demanded that new patterns of engagement were enacted; and this was a demand that, by virtue of particular individuals working within English Heritage, was subsequently acknowledged. In the past five years, the CCGG has initiated a number of projects relating to both the Garth and the wider village of Cawood, including qualitative community surveys; three 'mole-hill' surveys with local children; three history/finds days; two geophysical surveys; a landscape survey; a topographical survey; core-sampling; an ecology survey; newt protection training; an access audit; the installation of four benches and a bridge; archival research; a historical guide to the village; an A-Z of Cawood; Cawood Craft Festival exhibitions; a management plan; oral histories; filming and photography; a web site;[2] visits to other community heritage groups; a mammal discovery day; and pond-clearing, meadow raking and path maintenance working parties (Figure 4.1).

In contrast to generic depictions of 'community' as being consensual, 'good', and problem-free, the negotiations and debates underpinning these activities – notwithstanding those occurring between the CCGG and various institutional bodies – were often fraught. Indeed, one of the key messages of this volume is that those relationships *internal* to a community group are also problematic, *contra* both policy assumptions and the ideals often espoused by community activists themselves. We want to include those dissenting voices, which in this case study can be seen through the aspirations surrounding the management of the Garth, ranging from pleas to do nothing at all, to desires to limit interference to the installation of ade-

4.1. Resistivity surveying by the Cawood community on the Garth. [Photo: M. Brearley]

quate paths and seating, to appeals for picnic benches, barbe-que areas and camping facilities, to proposals for new buildings, such as a village hall, and car-parking facilities on the Garth (CCGG 2004). This range of aspirations means that they cannot all be afforded recognition – a pluralist solution is simply impossible, as 'nothing at all' is not compatible with new buildings and car-parking within the same geographical space. The community-wide survey instigated by the CCGG in 2004 revealed that disparate individuals and communities *within* the wider Cawood community were vying for parity of participation. The CCGG, then, who as a group are defined by a desire to lead in the management of the Garth in the wider community, were granted the power to mediate a range of demands and aspirations. The difficulty of adjudicating the more extreme aspirations was, however, more or less avoided in this instance because the CCGG is not afforded the equal status of 'full partner' with heritage professionals. The overriding say regarding proposals for new buildings on the Garth currently still lies with English Heritage. Thus, while these different groups within the village continue to be invested with competing and emotionally-charged notions of value and meaning, the wider politics of heritage ensure that they never feature significantly in the decision-making process.

The socio-demographic profile of Cawood is largely white and middle-class, with 99% identifying as 'white', according to National Statistic ethnicity categories, and 37% employed within National Statistic Socio-economic Levels 1 and 2 (managerial/professional), which is 10% higher than the national average, thereby associating with statistically constructed social class categories I and II. As Hodges and Watson (2000: 239) point out, this demographic is likely to bring with it a wealth of skills, networks and managerial competence conducive to the organisation and overseeing of large-scale projects, including the fund-raising aspects of the Cawood community work. Their reflections on Nether Poppleton, a case study similar to that of Cawood, led Hodges and Watson to conclude that considerable networking, communication and organisational skills – and time – are crucial for community-based action, and they went on to question this reality for community groups that do not find themselves in the advantageous position of economic affluence, or, to put it bluntly, in the privileged social position of the white middle-class. Our final case study for this chapter therefore takes us to Castleford, West Yorkshire, a post-industrial town attempting to overcome social and economic marginalisation.

Recognition and misrecognition in Castleford,
West Yorkshire

Castleford, near Leeds in West Yorkshire, is predominantly white and working-class, often measuring within the bottom 10% in many indices of poverty in England (Drake 2008). Originally a Roman settlement, Castleford became a significant industrial centre in the eighteenth century as a result of the large coal, sand and clay deposits associated with the confluence of the two navigable rivers on which Castleford sits. Coal mining was the dominant industry, but glass and pottery manufacture were also significant. Tailoring and sweet factories became important throughout the twentieth century, as these industries situated themselves in the town to attract the labour of the wives and daughters of mineworkers. A chemical industry and flour milling also developed in the town. Like many northern English towns, de-industrialisation has been a significant experience in the latter part of the twentieth century, starting with the closure of the potteries in the 1960s and, more recently, the closing of the chemical works in 2005, while the miners' strike of 1984-85 saw the loss of 3,000 jobs in the town. The impact of the strike is still felt in Castleford, and it is important to understand that the Thatcher government attacked not only the industry and the National Union of Mineworkers, but also well organised working-class communities. As part of de-industrialisation much of the built environment in Castleford has gone through radical changes and transformations. A great deal of what heritage mangers would identify as the industrial heritage of the town has been pulled down. Indeed, Castleford has never much featured on the radar of traditional accounts of heritage, with architect Nikolaus Pevsner in his survey of *The Buildings of England* dismissing it thus: 'what can the architectural recorder say about Castleford? There does not seem to be a single building in the centre of the town, which would justify mention' ([1959] 1986: 158).

Contrary, however, to the dictates of the AHD and architectural recorders, Castleford has been asserting its own understanding of heritage. The Castleford Heritage Trust (CHT, formally Castleford Heritage Group) began with a campaign in 1999 to get a clock put back on the Market Hall. This was mounted as a heritage campaign, much to the bemusement of the local council, as the clock to be 'restored' to its place on the market hall was a new one designed by a local artist. The argument was that the clock was about intangible heritage

– it was the place where people gathered to meet, and that was its significance, not its material authenticity (Drake 2008).

The CHT, like the CCGG, is a community within a community, and has been responsible for the creation of the Castleford Festival – a yearly event in July – whose primary audience is the residents of Castleford. This festival includes the mounting of exhibitions and stalls depicting aspects of local heritage and history in Castleford, as well as pageantry and marching with the old pit banners (Figure 4.2), maypole, musical performances, rag rug making, pottery painting demonstrations, art and poetry exhibitions, archaeological hands-on displays and other activities. The CHT also runs a range of projects concerned with the recording of individual and family histories that help to make personal and community linkages to the past via memory, reminiscence and performance. Through heritage lottery funding, the CHT has established offices, a permanent art gallery, a web site[3] and oral history archives, while also running services for local schools to provide resources for schoolchildren to learn about their local social and industrial history.

For many in the CHT and wider Castleford community, heritage is not *simply* the physical remains of the industrial landscape, nor primarily the Roman remains that still underlie modern Castleford. Nor is it its mining artefacts or pit banners and so forth. Intangible heritage is an important aspect in Castleford in two ways. First, much of what the CHT and other community members define as heritage are intangible events such as memories, oral histories, dances, music, industrial knowledge and workplace skills such as pottery painting. This does not mean that they reject 'tangible' or traditional forms of heritage, but that they see heritage as embracing intangible events and cultural expressions as well. Nor does this inclusion of the intangible reflect the absence of industrial material remains. Rather, it is an organic sense of what community heritage is – a view of heritage at odds with the AHD. Indeed, the idea of intangible heritage is not one that is readily understandable within the contexts of British heritage policy. As we have demonstrated elsewhere (Smith and Waterton 2008), the

4.2. The closing parade of the Castleford Heritage Festival, 2004. [Photo: L. Smith]

failure of the UK government to ratify the Intangible Cultural Heritage Convention rests on the inability of UK policymakers to see the relevance of 'intangible' heritage for Britain. The second way that intangible heritage is expressed in Castleford is in the degree to which community itself is seen as heritage. In oral histories and interviews collected with residents of Castleford, there is a strong sense that community, and the social networking, support and pride underpinning and creating that community, is also heritage. Heritage is defined as the set of social values that underpin and define the Castleford community, and which the CHT sees itself as 'preserving' and passing on to future generations. In particular, the Castleford festival, identified as a 'heritage' event, *is* heritage. It is:

> Important as it is showing everyone what it means to belong to a community – what's past and what's present. (CF49)

Opportunity for different groups in Castleford to get involved in one annual project. Gives children something to remember whey they get older. Memory jogger for older people. (CF7)

Not too sure – it may be a case of *producing* heritage and creating something now ... (CF17)

That we are proud of our heritage and want to celebrate it. We are building for the future. (CF64)

Heritage is also something that you actively undertake in Castleford. Possessing and looking at artefacts and other tangible aspects of heritage is not 'heritage' as such. Rather heritage is doing, as one member of the CHT pointed out: 'what is a heritage artefact or place if it is not being used: it is nothing and valueless' (Cas18 2004). Here, the value of heritage rests in the way an object or site of heritage is used in telling stories or in recalling past events and not passively gazed upon as static monuments.

The CHT is highly effective locally in helping generate a sense of community pride, and the organisation grew out of this need to redefine and reassert community identity in the face of de-industrialisation, continuing economic and social marginalisation, and government plans for regeneration (Drake 2004). What is important is the degree to which the CHT – and the way it defines and uses 'heritage' – is seen to represent the Castleford community. The representational power of traditional, organised labour has been significantly sidelined since the Miners' Strike, and with the class credentials of New Labour entirely suspect, structured formal community representation was deficient in Castleford. Further, in 1974, local government restructuring and centralisation saw Castleford lose its local council as it merged into the greater Wakefield Metropolitan District Council (Drake 2008). Local residents were concerned to ensure that their voice was heard and safeguarded in the execution of regeneration policies. The

CHT, and heritage more generally, has become significant in asserting 'that community does matter' (CF65). To some degree, the CHT has filled the representational void left by the disenfranchising of the Trade Unions under Thatcher. In Castleford, Trades Unions not only represented labour, but pursued social and cultural agendas. The CHT and heritage has come to fill part of the representational gap, and the CHT, through the festival and other activities it runs and supports, is actively attempting to legitimise the social justice aspirations and agendas of the wider Castleford community.

The representational importance and nuances of both heritage and the CHT is illustrated in an example that many heritage professionals may at first find inconsequential. In 2003, archaeologists discovered an archaeologically significant Iron Age chariot burial near Castleford. Drake (2008) reports that the burial was initially named the 'Ferrybridge' Chariot after a nearby landmark. However, the burial, but not the landmark, occur within the boundaries of Castleford. After much debate with the archaeological team in charge of the burial it was renamed the Ferry Fryston chariot burial. This may seem a trivial renaming, but it was important for the CHT and the local community in asserting their control over heritage resources. Control, here, is about how Castleford is represented and who is doing the representing.

Within Castleford the CHT has been highly successful; however, a significant issue for many members of the CHT has been the tensions that exit between their idea of heritage and the AHD (Smith 2006). These tensions have affected their ongoing funding opportunities and the degree to which government policymakers within the regeneration programme listen to their concerns and aspirations. Not only does the community not have ready access to the resources and skills of power identified by Hodges and Watson (2000), they are systematically excluded from a range of resources of power and influence by their representation of community identity. Their sense of heritage is misrecognised and misunderstood by governments, heritage agencies and other policymakers and state agencies simply because it does not conform to the AHD. Support for the CHT has come from individual heritage professionals, and while this support is important and vital, it pales in the face of the way the AHD is used to regulate and govern the legitimacy afforded to the heritage claims of Castleford. The point to be made here about community archaeology and/or heritage projects is that there is a systemic policy process that actively works to obscure the representational politics of heritage *regardless* of individual professional action. More to the point, however, the politics of heritage are obscured because the representations of Castleford simply cannot be seen, let alone understood, by state institutions and their policymakers trained and working in a system that defines heritage as material, 'old' and aesthetically worthy. Although the Cawood community itself had trouble in asserting their sense of heritage, the fact that their community identity was represented by a Castle Garth, as much as their socio-demographic profile, meant that they always had a better chance of being heard than the CHT. The CHT, of course, are not alone. There are many communities whose use of heritage to represent their collective identities will be misrecognised simply because it is too different from dominant and consensual assumptions about the nature and meaning of heritage. In multicultural Britain, the opportunity for community heritage to be misrecognised or rendered invisible remains significant (see Hall 1999; Littler & Naidoo 2005 for further discussion).

Conclusion

This chapter has considered a range of case studies, from Indigenous Australia to local community groups in the UK. The particulars of why and how each group engages and uses heritage and archaeology are obviously different in each case. This difference has often been cited within heritage and archaeological practice as something that means that we must deal with community archaeology/heritage projects on a case-by-case basis. While to some extent this may be true, it has tended to result in a failure to learn from the *collective* experiences of communities and heritage professionals who work together. It also helps facilitate the extent to which systemic issues are ignored or go unidentified. This ignorance means that heritage professionals engaging with communities make the mistake of assuming that their individual participation and support equates to the recognition of community interests. While we have been arguing that heritage professionals often hold a powerful place in Western societies, due partly to the authority given to them as intellectuals and partly to the fact that heritage policy and legislation explicitly recognise their expertise, individual action is not always enough. This is not to say that as individuals we should desist from engaging with communities. What we *are* saying is that we need to understand that as heritage professionals we hold dual positions in the process – both as individuals, with individual interests and agendas, but also as representatives and participants in wider social policy processes. Individual heritage professionals can be sidelined as much as communities if they deviate from the authorised processes in which they are enmeshed. Such occurrences do not help the communities we are engaging with, nor do they necessarily help the careers of professionals. It is important to appreciate and recognise the political networks that community archaeology and heritage sits within. In engaging with communities, heritage professionals cannot escape becoming implicated in the politics of recognition, but this is not something we should shy away from. Rather, the politics of recognition, the nature of dissonance and the relationship between heritage, identity and memory identified in this and previous chapters offer a way of understanding the wider significance of professional engagement with community interests. More importantly, these issues help us to acknowledge what is at stake for both communities and heritage professionals.

5

Museums and communities

Introduction

Community engagement by archaeologists and other heritage professionals is an ongoing process. However, engagement often stops when the 'dig' or other project ends. This sudden cessation may be entirely acceptable to all parties, but sometimes, and for some communities, it is not. This may be the case when communities have invested not only time and emotional energy into a project, but may also see the project as part of wider processes of ongoing identity expression and recognition. In these contexts the ending of a project, and thus engagement with communities of expertise, can be quite bewildering and frustrating. However, engaging with communities is an ongoing process that can be as important as the outcomes of the project itself. This process should be about equitable and respectful exchanges of dialogue undertaken with critical awareness of the wider contexts within which both communities and experts are operating.

A consideration of museums and communities is a useful point from which to consider the idea of community engagement as an ongoing relationship. This is because it is museums, at the end of excavations or other projects, who must take responsibility for curating and interpreting the collected data. When this data is also a community's heritage, communities must often then redevelop contacts and relationships with museum staff or new communities of expertise. This can be frustrating as communities re-engage with a process that inevitably impedes and frustrates community aspirations. A review of the literature on museum and community engagement reveals that this community of heritage experts shares many of the issues and concerns identifiable within the literature on 'community archaeology'. This reinforces our point that there are systemic issues associated with engagement, and heritage professionals need to open dialogue with each other and exchange views, practices and insights about the processes of community engagement and its consequences.

The community 'debate' in museums

Museums and their staff, like other heritage professionals, engage and interact with a range of different communities in a variety of ways and for different purposes. Museums may consult various communities about the content of new exhibitions, and these communities may range from those represented by 'Friends of ...' groups, volunteers, patrons, and other communities of museum visitors. They may also include 'special interest' communities, such as local communities or those sharing ethnic, cultural, religious, gender, age affiliations and so forth, communities based on explicit social or political agendas, or those sharing particular social or political experiences (see Mason 2005; Watson 2007 for further discussion). Communities may also be the subject of outreach and other educational programmes (Hooper-Greenhill 2007), be invited to use space within museums to mount their own temporary exhibitions (Szekers 2002), or develop and run their own museums. Significant examples of community or community-based museums include ecomuseums (Davis 1999) and Indigenous keeping-places and cultural centres (Kelly & Gordon 2002; Simpson 2007). Communities can also engage in protracted disputes with museums over the curation and retention of certain cultural artefacts, such as the Parthenon marbles, Benin Bronzes or human remains (Hamilakis 1999; Fforde et al. 2002; ARM n.d.).

Of particular significance to museums and their engagement with communities are social inclusion policies and practices, with the lead strategic agency in the UK, the Museums, Libraries and Archives Council (MLA), recently identifying such issues as key drivers of relevance to society (Crooke 2008: 418). Like other areas of the heritage and cultural sector, museums in the UK have been required to broaden their audiences. These policies have seen an escalating engagement with an increasing range of communities by museums. Traditionally, visitors to museums, like visitors to most traditional heritage sites (such as castles, country houses, archaeological monuments and so forth), are predominantly white, well-educated and middle-class and tend towards either the retired or those with children (Merriman 1991; Swain 2007). One of the aims of social inclusion initiatives has been to increase the range of communities who visit museums, galleries, heritage sites and cultural events. Such a construction of social inclusion would see Kawashima's (2006: 56) example of a classical orchestra playing in a shopping mall or the increase of visitor numbers from traditionally excluded communities (such as African-Caribbean British communities, Pakistani British, working-class communities etc.) as evidence of social inclusion at play. However, such ideas of social inclusion, and the sorts of community engagement that flow from this, are better understood as acts of cultural or social assimilation.

Museums and exclusion

Traditionally, museums have been viewed as institutions of public enculturation (Macdonald 2003: 5). The development of public museums in the nineteenth century occurred in a context that also saw the creation of the nation-state, and museums became immersed in the project of cementing and expressing national identity and nationalism (Bennett 1995). Modernist ideas of progress and scientific rationality, together with a liberal sense of pastoral care, underpinned the authority of museums to represent, regulate and pronounce upon national identity and to act as agents in the moral and social improvement of a nation's citizenry (Bennett 1995; Whitehead 2005). Museums also have a central and defining role as educators, and concerns with how museums educate, and how visitors learn, during the museum visit dominate much of this literature (Falk & Dierking 2000; Kelly 2004; Hooper-Greenhill 2007). More recent policy references to notions of 'community' as an ideal for invoking positive social change have meant that museums now also need to demonstrate their role in creating cohesion and inclusion (Crooke 2008: 417). In this context, the authority afforded to museums as arbitrators of appropriate taste, cultural value and national identity, together with a deeply ingrained sense of their educational role, has meant that social inclusion within museum practice has tended towards strategies that aim at bringing the excluded 'into the fold'. Indeed, as Tlili (2008) reports, social inclusion has become blurred with marketing issues, so that hitting numerical targets, which are measurable and related to funding, has tended to dominate approaches to social inclusion. Sara Selwood's (2006) analysis of increasing visitor numbers following the implementation of social inclusion strategies suggests that such policies have simply succeeded in attracting repeat visits from the same socio-economic groups. Moreover, social inclusion policy implementation is frequently relegated to particular officers or units within museums, and thus can be sidelined rather than integrated holistically into the institution – it becomes a gesture or an exercise in box-ticking (Tlili 2008). This approach to inclusion never really challenges the values and social and cultural functions of museums, because it does not question why certain communities are, or feel, excluded.

As Sandell (2003) observes, social inclusion requires a considerable shift in thinking about the relationship of museums to society, as well as a challenge to the idea of the expert (see Dodd and Sandell 2001 for further debate). The degree to which museums can and do present excluding narratives is well documented. Cash Cash (2001) argues that Indigenous identity and cultural knowledge can become refashioned through museum displays so that they become appropriated by national narratives, or neutralised and replaced by institutionally sanctioned narratives and knowledge. Similarly, Porter (1996) has noted that women's experiences are often obscured through the normative assumptions made about the importance of women's history that underwrite the collecting and interpreting strategies of museums. Labour history is another area that can be poorly translated into curatorial practices (Oliver & Reeves 2003), while the representation of experiences and identities of disability has also been critically examined (Dodd et al. 2004). Multiculturalism is another area currently presenting challenges to inclusive museums (Sandell 2007). These are just a few examples of the range of communities of interest who are questioning the representational role of museums and demanding that they take an active position on challenging discrimination based on, for example, ethnicity, class, gender, sexual preference, disability, religious affiliation, or age.

Uncritical approaches to social inclusion will simply see the recreation of universalist stories of nation being asserted to those who feel excluded from those narratives in the first place. What is achieved by this construction of 'social inclusion' – that is, encouraging more people from working-classes or ethnic minorities into visiting museums or traditional heritage sites – is the assimilation of a more diverse audience into the white middle-class and elite values that tend to underpin traditional museum and heritage displays. The term 'integration' is often used in social inclusion debates and policy initiatives, but 'integration' is simply another word for assimilation. In much the same way as policy language such as 'tolerance' conjures up an image of a patronising *allowance* by dominant groups for those who find themselves in a subordinate position, so the phrase 'integration' implies a one-way process, wherein the excluded are 'educated' into normative and politically dominant historical and heritage values and narratives. What is missing in this process, and in the language used to describe it, is respect for social and cultural diversity. Debates about 'integration' are always 'top-down' and never 'bottom-up', so that what may be important about history and heritage, and what they might mean to excluded communities, is not on the agenda. What is

107

interesting in the social inclusion debate is the lack of concern to get people from white middle-class or elite socio-economic categories visiting working-class, ethnic minority or other excluded or contentious forms of heritage. This means that currently social inclusion is *not* about respecting or understanding diversity. Rather, it is about disseminating and assimilating authorised historical and heritage narratives to a wider audience. What is also interesting is the apparent assumption that this broader audience would actually be interested in such narratives in any case.

Museums and inclusion

Social inclusion has the potential to occur only when the historical and contemporary experiences of exclusion are acknowledged, and the diversity of community identities within the nation is recognised and incorporated into museum narratives. This sort of inclusion will occur only through critically and politically aware community engagement. As Newman and McLean (2006) argue, the impact that museums have on identity means that they can be a positive vehicle for social inclusion. In fact, Sandell (2002: 3) asserts that museums have the responsibility to combat social inequality. The turn to New Museology in the UK, and the social history movement in the US, has seen increasing concern within museums to develop relationships with communities that attempt to challenge power relations (see Vergo 1989; Karp 1992; Handler & Gable 1997; Ross 2004). This responsibility means not only engaging with and 'owning' political agendas within curatorial practice, but also allowing room for communities to assert and drive their own agendas. As Fyfe (1996) notes, although museums are implicated in the reproduction of the social order, this does not mean that it is not actively contested. Communities are not waiting passively, 'out there' within the public body, to be identified and 'included'.

Museum research has revealed that museum visitors are active agents in the way that they engage with museum exhibitions (Bagnall 2003; Longhurst et al. 2004). Further, 'education' is not always given as the main motivation for visiting. As Orr (2004) notes, the reasons for visiting are not easily revealed, and a range of diffuse motivations have been recorded. While learning *does* occur at museums it can be incidental (Katriel 1997), and research by Doering suggests that exhibitions that *confirm* visitors' worldviews are more often identified as satisfactory in visitor surveys (cited in Orr 2004). Interviews conducted with visitors as part of wider research projects at social history museums, house museums and at exhibitions marking the 1807 bicentenary also support the idea that people tend to confirm their views and ideas at museums (Smith 2006, 2008b). What this shows is that there is a range of identity and memory 'work' that people undertake while visiting museums. Moreover, the relationship between museums and communities is highly complex, multi-layered and continually changing. Museums are places that communities use to represent and communicate their sense of belonging to other members of their community or to external audiences, and have come to be defined as places people use to 'think with' (Fyfe & Ross 1996: 148; Crooke 2007). They are also used as places to remember and reminiscence, and to pass these reminiscences on to family members, and are places where people may find expression for their identity and sense of place (Urry 1996; Smith 2006). Thus, visiting can be understood as a performance in which certain identities are being expressed. This performance can occur both in terms of the actual act of visiting and/or the way visitors engage with, and construct meaning for, certain exhibitions (Smith 2006; Dicks 2008). The point is that the relationship between museums, their audiences and communities is not passive. Museums, like other places of heritage, become sites of mediation and authorisation.

This relationship is encapsulated in Crooke's (2007: 131) statement that it 'is people who bring the value and consequence to objects and collections; as a result, if a museum cannot forge associations with people it will have no meaning'. This resonates with the statement by a Castleford community member cited in Chapter 4 that objects have no value unless they are being used. The objects museums conserve and exhibit have, of course, no intrinsic value; it is people who invest them with meaning and symbolic power. The relationship between museum staff, archaeologists and non-museum heritage professionals is made complex by the way we use heritage to undertake a range of social and cultural 'work', as discussed in Chapters 1-4. In some ways, we may say that museums 'create' communities in the sense that the representational authority of museums helps to validate and legitimise community identity claims and all that flows from this. However, this complex cultural and social relationship is made more difficult by a range of issues discussed below.

'Acquistive relationships'[1]

The ability of expert communities to talk past, and misunderstand, the communities of interest with which they work is significant. One of the fundamental reasons for this rests with the fetishisation of material objects (Macdonald 2002). The history of museums is centred on an obsession with 'the thing', and the curation and celebration of aesthetics is still argued by some to be the primary aim of museums (Appleton 2007). Despite support in the museums literature and curatorial practice for a community agenda, the authority and nature of the institutions within which curators work mean that they will inevitably have the final say on, or responsibility for, how artefacts and other exhibits are used and the meanings constructed around them in displays (Witcomb 2003). The issue, however, is how that authority is *used*. Indeed, the shift that Sandall (2003) calls for, and which was the aim of the New Museology, is yet to be realised in museum practice. This is demonstrated in the degree of hostility and bemusement that is often expressed over repatriation debates between museums, particularly in England, and Indigenous peoples (Chalmers 2003; Jenkins 2003; Brothwell 2004). Following reviews of policy and legislation in 2003-4, British museums have been the focus of renewed requests by Indigenous Australian communities for the return of human remains (DCMS 2003; Smith 2004b). The bemused response such requests receive rests on the inability of museum curators and archaeologists to understand that objects can and do exist within competing spheres of meaning. However, this bemusement is not confined to debates between Indigenous peoples and museums. Other oft-cited disputes include continuing repatriation debates over the Parthenon marbles, the Benin bronzes, and the successful repatriation of the Lakota Ghost Shirt from Scotland. However, such disputes do not occur only between nations, but can also crop up at sub-national community levels. In Castleford, the CHT (discussed in Chapter 4) requested the return of some Roman artefacts from regional museums. During the 1970s, and as a result of local government reorganisation, museum collections of Roman cultural material that archaeologists had excavated and collected at sites around the town were removed to regional museums. The CHT had asked that some of these items be included in a community exhibition to be held at Castleford. This met with some resistance, and the CHT was told that these artefacts could not be returned as they were 'too valuable' (Drake 2008: 69). The value perceived here by the museums in question rested on an assumption about the innate or essentialised archaeological or informational value that they are assumed to possess – their fetishisation. Alison Drake, chair of the CHT, observes:

> The CHT members emphasised that the collections were, to them, worthless if the community to which they belong never saw them. Council officers stated that the museum service had a duty to preserve the collection for future generations, so the group asked which generations in particular were seen as the focus of the work of the museum service, as there were now three generations in Castleford who had never seen the items in question (2008: 69).

We see here a misunderstanding of the point Crooke (2007) made about the relationships between objects, communities and representation. At the time of the request the items were not on display but held in museum vaults and, thus, to the Castleford community were worthless – their value resting on the inability of the community to use them to create and represent their own community messages and meanings. In this instance, this issue was resolved to the satisfaction of both the CHT and museum professionals. However, it is useful to note that the artefacts here *were* being used by the museum, even though they were not currently part of a public display. The possession and control of artefacts by museums is as much about proclaiming identity for professionals or institutions as it is for other communities. As artefacts become 'inalienable possessions', surrendering the possession of those things that historically constitute the museum and the museum's reason for existence, challenges institutional and professional identity. It requires museum staff to question and evaluate their own identities and roles as museum experts. Further, as museum staff are also members of wider social or cultural communities, any involvement with communities of interest may also require staff to examine their own community identities, and the values and cultural assumptions that underpin them. Community engagement requires a fundamental philosophical shift in the museum community's values and sense of belonging, and this is something that needs more than a change in policy. This shift is not easy because, as with the communities with which museums work, the museum community is itself disparate. Other community members will of course challenge moves by individual curators that threaten the museum community's identity. More importantly, however, challenges will also come from other communities as well, particularly those that are comfortable with the ways in which museums represent them.

As Davis (2007: 57) points out, advocacy by museum curators on behalf of excluded communities can leave curators very exposed. For instance, exhibitions about, and institutional policies on, engagement with Indigenous Australia at the National

Museum in Canberra saw that museum embroiled in very public and politically charged 'history wars' over the significance and nature of colonial history (Casey 2007). The *Enola Gay* exhibition discussed in Chapter 3 is another example of the way staff can be exposed to pressure. Museums and their staff will be criticised for being 'political' or even 'politically correct' (Macdonald 1998; Szekeres 2002). This charge of political correctness has become a mark of derision for those professionals who act to advocate and support community-based work. A meaningless phrase, it simply denotes discomfort with the political agendas being pursued. Another often-cited criticism is that museums and their curators have belittled their authority by pandering to public entertainment. 'Infotainment', or 'edutainment', like 'political correctness', are shorthand phrases expressing discomfort with changes within the museum community. In both cases the use of these terms or phrases is a response to threats to the core values of museum practice, philosophy and identity. These core values are that museums can be 'objective' and should primarily be about top-down 'education' and enculturation. However, while community engagement does expose museum staff to such critique, failure to engage while assuming the identity of authoritative expert is no less political and open to exposure. Museum staff, like other heritage professionals, are engaged in a cultural process of meaning-making that has consequences. Thus, criticism and entanglement in dissonant disputes are, as argued in Chapter 3, part of the territory heritage professionals occupy.

One of the significant issues facing the development of museum-community relationships is the bewildering, shifting and complex nature of communities, and this statement holds true for both communities of interest and museum communities. The museums literature often points to the difficulty of identifying who museums should contact in particular communities. How museums *know* who really represents a community and, as communities are disparate entities, how museums *evaluate* which individuals or organisations really represent broad community issues, are worrying concerns. So daunting

113

and difficult are these issues that many museums tend to focus on the clearly defined, well-organised and vocal communities (Watson 2007: 2). Communities, however, also face similar issues when engaging with the institutional nature of the museum. This is because institutions such as museums can not only appear very impersonal, but can also be difficult for an uninitiated community to engage with. Community outreach officers or units and individual curators may provide the desired links between communities and the museum. However, such links are inevitably fragile and mutable as individuals move jobs or as museums undergo restructuring, and thus the faces of community contact officers change. These may seem obvious observations, but the point is that although community engagement is often scary and risky for heritage professionals and museums, and while it leaves staff exposed to professional criticism, it can also be *equally* scary and risky for communities and their representatives, who can be as exposed as the museum/ heritage professional.

Museums, in their desire to consult with communities about the development of exhibitions, or as they open up exhibition space to community-led exhibitions and so forth, can place considerable pressure on individuals. Interviews with community groups involved in the development of exhibitions marking the 2007 bicentenary of Britain's abolition of its slave trade report on the considerable pressure that individuals were put under by museums to represent quite disparate and diffuse communities (Fouseki 2008). Within museums, as in many state bureaucracies, committees form a particular way of consulting upon, negotiating and debating issues. Committees are often highly structured, operate to formal (if often unwritten) rules and protocols and, above all, based on the idea of *representation* whereby individuals are charged to represent the views of interested parties in the issues or problems under discussion. Community consultation that follows the committee model will often see the appointment of individual representatives from identified communities. Some communities and their representatives will find committee work familiar and comfortable, but this is not the case for all. Community representatives interviewed as part of research on the 2007 bicentenary reported not only that too much pressure and responsibility was placed on them to represent the needs of diverse and mutable communities, but also that they often felt isolated and exposed in such committees. Moreover, these individuals also become exposed to community criticism if (or when) exhibitions or other projects do not live up to wider expectations.

Part of the problem lies with the idea of 'consultation'. Relationships between museums and communities are often based on the idea that communities are there simply to consult with about the content or aims of an exhibition, outreach programme or other project. Sheila Watson characterises this as an 'acquisitive relationship' (2007: 2). Indeed communities and their representatives can be 'collected' by museums to help legitimise exhibition content and policy development. It is all too easy for consultation to become part of the social inclusion 'tick-box' phenomenon. Witcomb (2003: 89) also sees the idea of consultation as limited, and offers James Clifford's idea of museums as 'contact zones' to mitigate this problem, in which contemporary and historical, moral and political meanings are negotiated and mediated. Dialogue is key here, and as the balance of power in such dialogues will be in favour of the museum, a commitment to *negotiation* rather than consultation in these exchanges is vital. Indeed, the idea of a 'community of practice' is one that has been advocated within the museums literature (Kelly & Gordon 2002; Kelly 2004; Crooke 2005, 2007). This refers to the idea of collective learning through working towards a common goal, resulting in practices that are reflective of both the goal and development of a social relationship built over time (Kelly & Gordon 2002: 153). While Kelly and Gordon argue that museums professionals should act as facilitators for community expression through museums, Whitcomb (2003: 101) sees the role of curator as more complicated, arguing that it involves a responsibility for defining the community to be represented. This should not be seen, Whitcomb argues, as a repressive exercise of power, but rather one of positive civic reform that legitimises the idea of cultural diversity.

One of the criticisms often voiced by community groups is that once the exhibition is in place the relationship with the museum ends or gradually dissolves, while others note that they feel like a resource that the museum will use each time it needs to undertake community consultation. These situations contradict any sense of 'relationship'. While it may be hard for museum staff to maintain relationships or communities of practice with the sometimes very wide ranging and disparate communities with which they work, these 'relationships' occur anyway. If we accept that museums are not simply treasure-houses full of 'stuff', or *only* about 'top-down' educating and learning, but rather sites of meaning-making, then relationships with communities become central to museum practice. Even if we accept the traditional model of a museum, the consequence of which is the enculturation and the making of 'good' cultured citizens, the museum still establishes relationships with communities – albeit inclusive ones with traditional museum visitors and relationships of exclusion and de-legitimisation with many others. Community links do not end with the opening of the exhibition; once opened and visited, exhibitions do cultural and social 'work' – they tell stories, convey messages and values, and people interact and engage with exhibitions in a variety of ways. The messages audiences take away will have consequences for communities, and thus dialogue about those consequences needs to be maintained between communities and museums.

The process of engagement can be as important, and sometimes more important, than the practical outcome of a heritage project. It is the *process* as much as the end product that is about the creation, maintenance and safeguarding of heritage and the identities and social values that flow from this. As Crooke (2005) discusses in relation to the development of community exhibitions in Northern Ireland, the exhibitions were *part of* a process of celebration and remembrance, or a means to

an end. In the process of developing exhibitions, group meet-
ings were held and discussions and dialogue occurred within
the community that saw the development of community pride,
self-esteem, and the cementing of community social networks.
If we accept the argument advanced in Chapter 2 that heritage
is a process of meaning-making, then as museums and other
heritage professionals become entwined in this process they
cannot help but become *active* players. The decision then rests
with heritage professionals as to whether they become voices of
'authentification' and authorisation in this process or something more creative and engaging.

Conclusion

Although this chapter addresses the relationship between museums and communities, the point we have stressed is that all
heritage professionals are engaged in ongoing relationships
with communities that do not end with the 'dig' or the pre-
served or conserved 'monument'. As communities of experts
engage with communities of interest, they become active advocates and players within the cultural and social processes of
'heritage-making', and the (re)creation and maintenance of cultural values and narratives. This engagement is unavoidable
and it becomes important for experts to 'own' the political and
social agendas, assumptions and values that they bring to
these engagements as much as it is for communities to 'own'
theirs. Community relationships are difficult and fraught, and
they do not exist to tick a box in social policy implementations
or to legitimise the agendas and practices of heritage professionals. If that is all they do, then the potential of community
engagement can only be defined as social and cultural assimilation or integration. It is important to remember that communities and heritage professionals operate within an unequal
framework, and thus communities may sometimes seek to use
experts to legitimise community identity and aspirations, and
they will do so because of the authority of expertise and the
legitimising power of the institutions within which experts

work. The response of the expert to this use will inevitably depend on the political agendas and sympathies of that expert. Indeed, how and why heritage professionals engage with communities will always depend on the institutional and individual political and social agendas that experts work with – whether following social inclusion or other public policy defined by government or more personal agendas. Community relationships will be framed by a whole range of social, cultural and political agendas. This framework, however, need not be set in stone, nor necessarily set and led by communities of experts. Rather, if we envisage engagement with communities as an ongoing relationship, then it becomes mutually beneficial that part of that engagement should include the active and self-conscious negotiation of the social and political agendas being pursued.

6

Digital communities

Introduction

Recent decades have seen a proliferation of debate surrounding the significance of the internet and computer-mediated communication (CMC). Simultaneously, awareness that common interests, rather than geographic proximity, would underlie the meaning of 'community' has developed (Licklider & Taylor, cited in Jones 1997: 10). It should come as no surprise that there has been an emerging breadth of literature that seeks to bring together these cultural formations and examine the possibility of 'online community'. From the early 1990s onwards, a growing number of books, articles and conferences have begun to realign a concept traditionally associated with senses of belonging and affective experiences derived from place-based and face-to-face encounters with the realm of CMC. This interest is not confined to the academy alone. Indeed, in 2006, *TIME* magazine signalled that the melding of more traditional notions of community with life online had, indeed, taken place with their pronouncement of 'You' as Person of the Year. In explanation, Grossman (2006) introduced the special section of that *TIME* edition with the following reflection:

> It's a story about community and collaboration on a scale never seen before. It's about the cosmic compendium of knowledge Wikipedia and the million-channel people's network YouTube and the online metropolis MySpace. It's about the many wresting power from the few and helping one another for nothing and how that will not only change the world, but also change the way the world changes.

Community had become, as Jones (1997: 10) predicted, no longer a place to *physically be,* but a metaphor for a new range of modes of interaction provided by the parameters of the internet.

Despite – or perhaps because of – this influx of interest, the idea of community online is still approached in many different ways. Some scholars lament a sense of loss, and cite the compression of time and space in the wake of modernising technology as a cause of breakdown of community ties (Watson 1997). Many more have begun to question the relevance of 'community' to contemporary society and dismiss that tinge of nostalgia commonly associated with it (Wellman & Gulia 1999: 169; Crang et al. 1999). Others still argue that the social changes occurring in relation to the internet are not dissimilar to those wrought by the telephone, television, fax etc., suggesting that there is nothing inherently new in the way social relations are defined and maintained (Kollock & Smith 1996). It is probably fair to say that there is no evidence for a wideranging acceptance of 'life online', nor a consensus for how it is to be understood. Quite the contrary, the concept of 'community' continues to be a notion that is venomously criticised and denied when used in association with the internet (Bakardjieva 2003: 293).

Regardless of the nuances of the above debate, this longstanding interest in the internet will inevitably impact upon the realm of heritage management. Electronic media, with their new resources and fields of communication, will decisively change the way we encounter heritage, conduct ourselves in relation to heritage and explore the responses of others. Moreover, it will have a significant impact on the ways in which heritage professionals engage with community groups and vice versa. It is therefore important to develop an understanding of what 'online community' means and how that sense of community is facilitated within the heritage sector. As the emergence of digital communities is a relatively recent phenomenon, the analysis offered in this chapter remains somewhat limited. Our aim is to provide a more general reflection on the negotiation of identity and community online, and examine some instances within which we see a semblance of 'community' emerging in association with heritage and archaeology websites. We will examine more generally how the emerging telecommunications of the 'information' and 'network' society have redefined our connections with community, not only in a technical sense, but politically and socially. Central to this chapter is the internet, a powerful vehicle for expression that is rapidly developing new social and cultural contexts where networks – both literally and metaphorically – are established, developed and sustained across machines, people and places (Boyd-Barrett 2004: 28). It is 'an emergent, ever-changing set of communicative practices that comprises temporary and shifting relationships, communities, organisations, and cultures' (Markham 1998: 221). Before an in-depth discussion of how the concept of digital communities plays out in the heritage sector is undertaken, it is first necessary to explore the idea of social networking and provide an overview of the mechanisms available to us online.

Social networking online

A basic premise of this chapter is that the concept of 'community' has been stretched out beyond the physical and re-imagined in connection with the more technologically sensitive concept of 'social network'. Often, this *stretching* is legitimised with reference to Benedict Anderson's (1983) notion of the 'imagined community', and the understanding that virtual communities, like 'real life' communities, are not forced to engage in face-to-face encounters, nor will they necessarily ever physically know each other. Nonetheless, a range of relationships can – and often will – develop online. Here, Anderson's (1983: 15) argument that 'communities are to be distinguished, not by their falsity/genuineness, but by the style in which they are imagined' has significant leverage. An important corollary is that 'virtual' and 'real life' communities are neither in opposition, nor in danger of one supplanting the other. Rather, social interactions that occur online are more likely to enhance a suite of 'real life' identities and relationships. The important point is that the advent of the internet has not instigated a new category of human interaction; rather, it has created a new *space*, or place, within which to analyse and observe a concept that has been exercising scholars for a considerable time.

Widespread interest in the overlap between the internet and society has triggered a proliferation of terms and phrases. The concept 'virtual community' is perhaps the most widely cited, and was first coined by Howard Rheingold (1993: 5), who proposed the following definition:

> Virtual communities are social aggregations that emerge from the Net when enough people carry on those public discussions long enough, with sufficient human feeling, to form webs of personal relationships in cyberspace.

Like much of the literature dealing with ideas of 'community', the language drawn upon to define the virtual counterpart often revolves around more traditional, geographical concepts such as 'neighbourhoods', 'settlements', 'frontiers', 'commons' and 'publics'. Perhaps the most evocative of these is 'frontier' (Rheingold 1993), which is often used to create a vision of an unregulated and unfettered social space opening up before us. Within that space, a liberating anonymity is created where we can 'hang out', meet people, exchange ideas, perform acts of writing ourselves and engage in virtual play using multiple, flexible identities (Molz 2004). Imagined as a utopian space, the internet is often described as a place within which to create narratives, histories and agendas that are no longer shaped by the state, institutions or academic voice (Ho 2007). Moreover, as Benwell and Stokoe (2006: 243) propose, this lack of impediments is suggestive of a world where people can do what they like, say what they like and be who they like, based upon the indeterminacy and transient nature of the internet. There has, however, been a vigorous and disparaging response to this

strong democratising storyline. For these scholars, online social engagements are often characterised as false, inauthentic
and totalising (Crang et al. 1999: 3 for a fuller discussion). The
freedom of the 'frontier', it would seem, is so palpable that
users will lose themselves in its endless textures and escape
into a constructed world free from the in-person, in-the-flesh
encounters of the real world (Wellman & Gulia 1999: 168). For
these scholars, there is little congruence between the sense of
community developing online and a nostalgically remembered
notion of 'community' associated with traditional, egalitarian
life.

Recently, scholars have begun to develop a critical account of
CMC. Here, virtuality is still conceived of as a heterogeneous
environment that is fluid and shifting, but it has come to be
imagined as something relatively stable. Common, here, is the
idea that while the internet may be used to gather and circu-
late information, it is also a tool that is deployed for
strengthening social ties within 'real life' communities
(Kavanaugh 1999: 10). This is mediated by the presence of
affective bonds that give rise to a *sense of virtual community*
(Blanchard and Markus 2004: 66). This sense of virtual community is something that is experienced and embodied,
engendering feelings of membership, influence, integration
and emotional connection (ibid.: 67-8). Markham (1998: 212-
13) demarcates three experiences of 'life online': (1) a tool for
information; (2) a place where relationships are made; and (3)
a way of being. Perhaps the most salient aspect of this broad-
ened understanding of social networking is that it is envisaged
as an embodied experience. Thus, while communication online
ostensibly takes place through text construction and electronic
exchange, this type of interaction also carries an embodied
status, or process of (re)embodying:

> The communicative interaction is not 'in' the machinery.
> It is rather shared between persons and interpreted by
> each interactant. We experience the system through our
> bodily systems, and we exchange this experience with

others through the communication of the network. The
traces of others are carried within us physically as we
experience together (Argyle & Shields 1996: 61).

Here, communication is metaphorically punctuated with non-
verbal, embodied elements and expressions (Markham 1998:
136). Within each interactional performance, we map our own
identities and understandings of 'self' and 'other' into the ter-
rain of cyberspace. In order to protect and maintain this sense
of virtual community, particular social behaviours and cues are
encouraged, which are in turn used to provide support, control,
boundaries, obligation and leadership (Dicks 2003: 188). Importantly, this understanding of life online reveals a place that
is enmeshed with a range of rules and regulations that pro-
duces a social world characterised by vast power imbalances
(Kollock & Smith 1999: 13). These areas for community engagement are policed, with consequences for those who 'cross
the line' or break the rules (Dicks 2003: 188). Far from the
utopian enterprise posited by less critical commentators, more
recent analyses of cyberspace reveal a social landscape that is
also politically complex, replete with class divisions, gender
imbalances and social negotiations previously heralded as ob-
solete (Nakamura 2000). As such, it is also a space that is as
much to do with inclusion and exclusion as the other case
studies examined in this book, and is thus susceptible to the
same arenas of conflict and misrecognition in and between
different community groups.

Inevitably, scholars have turned to questioning the role of
identity in cyberspace, and perhaps some of the most important
contributions come from those seeking to limit the distance
implied between 'real' identities and the apparent freedom of
'virtual' identities. If identity is, as many have argued, the way
in which we experience and understand ourselves, then *all*
identities are inevitably contingent, changing and constructed.
The notion of a virtual identity is simply harder to establish.
Despite this, the *potential* falseness of virtual identities – and
here scholars often conveniently forget the malleability of all

identities, real or otherwise – has forged a situation within which virtual identities are put at risk and characterised as unreal, inauthentic and inferior. In reality, these identities are no less fluid than everyday/real identities, which are themselves theorised as being discursively constructed and constituted. As Benwell and Stokoe (2006: 245, emphasis in original) point out:

> In this version of identity, 'virtual' becomes a red-herring: a moniker that perpetuates the myth of the authentic, stable and essential identity. With these arguments in mind, we may decide that 'virtual identity' is simply a prosaic term for the identity work that *happens* to occur online.

A general consensus has emerged that seeks to distinguish formations of 'community' from more general online gatherings, by extending definitions *beyond* a critical mass of active participants delineated by an engagement in ongoing discussions. While participation in such communities will undoubtedly include those who are adopting a passive style of participation (known as 'lurkers'), active participation remains an integral element. This understanding of 'virtual community' stands in contradiction to both the anonymity and totalising features often aligned with the virtual world, particularly in its attempts to construct a sense of trust, legitimacy and identity both *within* and *in relation* to a social group.

The internet

World Stats.com estimated that a total of 19.1% of the worlds' population are engaged in internet usage, based on data collected in 2007.[1] By comparison, figures collected in the United Kingdom in 2007 show that 61% of households have internet access. From these statistics, a sense of information inequality starts to emerge, which is further differentiated within the UK by educational and physical inabilities to work online (Bell

2001: 108-9). Suffice to say that the number of internet users, while staggeringly large in the Western world, is dominated by a user group that is predominantly white, male and middle-class (Nakamura 2000: 713). This is not dissimilar to the demographic profile of those involved in traditional or authorised heritage pursuits, at least in terms of class and ethnicity.

Before discussing the ways in which an interest in heritage and archaeology creates a sense of community *through* the internet, it is first necessary to briefly explore the variety of ways in which we encounter life online. This list includes asynchronous forms of online media, such as email, conferencing systems – including Usenet (a computer network discussion system), ECHO and the WELL – BBSs (Bulletin Board System), blogging, wikis, pod-casting, discussion forums and discussion lists. Of these, email and discussion lists are the most prevalent and revolve around what is called 'push' media, through which messages are sent to a range of recipients (Kollock & Smith 1999: 6). In the case studies explored in Chapter 4 the use of email worked to increase community participation and strengthen the diversity of social interaction. Discussions lists and forums concerned with archaeology and heritage projects are becoming increasingly visible online, and include forums such as *BAJR, Bad Archaeology: Leave Your Common Sense Behind, Britarch* and *The Digital Society of the Past.* Likewise, the possibility of building author-generated content like wikis exists, such as the *York Community Archaeology Wiki*, although the momentum for this has not yet taken hold (Hull, CBA, 17 August 2007). A range of synchronous types of communication, including text chat (Instant Messaging or real-time text chat), MUDs (Multiple User Domains), chat rooms and social networking are also available online. The WWW itself offers both synchronous and asynchronous modes of communication, and currently hosts an impressive array of community heritage/archaeology websites including *Friends of Thornborough Henges,* the *Friends of Skipwith Common*, the *Catalhöyük: Excavations of a Neolithic Höyük* website, *Community Archaeology Ltd*, and the *Honouring the Ancient Dead* network. MUDs are an attempt to introduce face-to-face communication to the virtual world and offer text-based, social virtual realities to multiple users in which embodied communication is simulated. MUD domains tend to be heavily policed, with high status subject positions marked out as 'Gods' and 'Wizards' in highly stratified social engagements (Kollock & Smith 1999: 7). The *Flaminia Project* is an example of an archaeologically based MUD that allows multiple users to assume avatars and 'wander' around a 3D reconstruction of an archaeological landscape (Pietroni & Forte 2007).

The idea that the internet can be a place in which to meet and interact with a range of people is borne out by the popularity of social networking phenomena such as MySpace and Facebook, alongside the emergence of user generated sites like YouTube and Flickr. YouTube, Facebook and MySpace regularly feature on the Top 25 visited sites globally, based upon the number of users visiting the site. YouTube was visited by 18.35% of internet users on 16 January 2008, with 5.465% visiting MySpace and 5.374% visiting Facebook.[2] As a collective, NetRatings (2006) estimates that the top ten social networking sites currently available grew by around 47% in just a year, reaching some 45% of active users in 2006. Similarly compelling are figures associated with active user accounts for both Facebook and MySpace, which boast 60 and 300 million active users respectively, with 150,000 and 230,000 new users signing up daily (Facebook 2007; MySpace 2007). This exciting growth has not escaped Facebook users, some of whom have formed specific groups that aim to analyse the emergence of online communities. Likewise, a cursory search through Facebook for groups concerned with archaeology and/or heritage will return over 500 instances of group formation around either topic. This interest in social networking has spanned popular, policy and academic contexts, and is now a subject that can now be found in a range of university prospectuses in the UK, Europe and the US.

Looking at life online

As Wellman and Gulia (1999: 174) point out:

> Emotional support, companionship, information, making arrangements, and providing a sense of belonging are all non-material social resources that are relatively easy to provide from the comfort of one's computer.

They are the sorts of resources frequently associated with real-life communities, and if these things can be sustained online, then, the logic follows, online relationships and interactions are capable of being realigned within the boundaries of community. If we accept that online communities *are* real communities, then how is the architecture of community created and sustained online?

One way in which it is done, as Donarth (1999) highlights, is the way identity is authenticated. He identifies useful markers present in any given email discussion list that users rely upon to transmit a sense of self. The importance of these identity markers is tied to the enduring image of the internet as a fraudulent and inauthentic environment with seemingly no recognised standards for reliability. In these instances users rely upon implicit markers to signal the veracity of their opinions and reputation, much of which is drawn from an email address line. Here, institutional affiliation can be derived from the virtual neighbourhood – domain or host – associated with an email address. For example, the authors' email addresses are: ls18@york.ac.uk and e.waterton@his.keele.ac.uk, where the virtual neighbourhoods can be read as york.ac.uk and keele.ac.uk respectively, thereby signifying an institutional affiliation with either the University of York or Keele University. Likewise, users frequently append their posts with a 'signature' they have set up in association with their email account, which generally lists their name, email, phone number and perhaps a personal website. This offers a sort of business card, or form of elaborate identity demarcation, which for other users provides depth, both in terms of time and information, that can be used to allay fears of deception (Donath 1999: 41). In a similar way, social tagging is used to demarcate a sense of personal identity:

> Social tagging, for example, is a way in which people can say to everybody else 'here are all the things on the internet that I like. You can check out my social tagging profile if you like. You can also check out all my links that I have created to all the interesting pages I think are good' … And that, in itself, is a really quick and easy way for a person to build up their identity and broadcast it to others (Hull, CBA, 17 August 2007).

Wellman and Gulia (1999: 172) suggest that while online interaction often sponsors specialised relationships concerned with information acquisition, rather than broadly based encounters, information exchange remains 'only one of many social resources that is exchanged on the Net'. Indeed, they argue that users are *also* looking for personal encounters that signify companionship and elements of social support. This is an observation shared by Hull (CBA, 17 August 2007), who notes:

> Often people are bound together by similar discussions, like metal detecting, for example, and they come to know each other and their online persona … they feel they know each other very well and the way they refer to each other becomes more and more casual and includes a lot of quite specific personal references.

The type of interaction anecdotally relayed by Hull falls into a category of interaction that Wellman and Guila (1999: 176) label as 'weak ties', which derive from the social and physical distance of communicating online. These weak ties are instigated across social networks developing online in a way that is *more* persistent than the strong ties we often experience in 'real life'. Consequently, Wellman and Gulia (1999: 183) are reluctant to see these weak ties as insignificant, pointing out that the 'vast majority of informal interpersonal ties are weak ties, whether they operate online or face-to-face'.

Britarch: a case study

At the beginning of 2008, the Britarch email discussion list had 1,438[3] subscribers, which consisted of both active and occasional users, and 'lurkers'. Despite the list being ostensibly about the exchange of information and discussion around archaeological issues, there does exist evidence of community. Across the archive, there is a developed sense of 'us' and communal grouping, along with the more than occasional reference to friendships established online (see BAP1, 2008; BAP2, 2008, BAP3, 2008), which indicates that the site is also used for something beyond information. This type of interaction reflects arguments developed by Wellman and Gulia (1999), who suggest that the accumulation of small acts of friendship, support and advice, readily visible by all who subscribe to the discussion list, will sustain the larger community. This is because each act sustains that sense of community, along with all its attendant requirements of reciprocity and mutual aid (ibid.: 178). The following succession of posts to the Britarch discussion list supports this line of argument:

> ... 'friends' only became friends as a result of my communications with Britarch during an hour of need. Furthermore, I have been greatly enheartened by list members not on my usual list of friends ... I could not have done this without the enduring and magnificent support from my more than virtual friends on Britarch (BAP2, 2008).

> ... I have no objection to John's or anyone else posting occasionally about other stuff – we all have moments in our lives when we need some support and where it comes from is not the point... We're not just archaeologists and interested parties, we're people too (BAP3, 2008).

If John can get a measure of support from his friends through Britarch then I personally don't see the problem (BAP4, 2008).

Although the extracts above were posted in close succession and triggered by a particular event, the observation to be made here is that what we see emerging is a social network stretching between friends, colleagues and acquaintances who do not, one would imagine, live in the same village, town or neighbourhood. Characterised by a sense of reciprocity, this exchange revolves around offering and receiving support, acknowledging a sense of friendship and instigating group attachment. In this instance, a common interest in archaeology, which is negotiated and expressed online, has become a meeting point through which a sense of community is facilitated. At the same time, the online community works to mediate and reinforce a particular idea of heritage that *means something* to that community group. As a discussion forum that operates through the CBA, this will carry significant implications for the wider heritage process because of the institutional authority invested with the CBA. First, it may challenge the concept of 'community' animating public policy, which currently advocates a management process that is as much about exclusion and elitism as it is about genuine community engagement. Second, however, it also offers a medium through which the archaeological community can strengthen their understanding of 'heritage' in the face of alternative perspectives by fostering a visible community of support and authority.

Ligali: a case study

As was noted earlier, the internet has failed to become the democratising force it was once thought it would be. A notable point from the case study above is that the online community sponsored by Britarch is that of the professional archaeologist – a community within the heritage sector that has traditionally enjoyed a position of privilege and power. Indeed, the most prevalent type of online community developing in relation to archaeology and heritage tends to be associated with the archaeological 'expert', where reputation and institutional affiliation matter. Thus, while it is theoretically possible for groups of people engaged in heritage projects to have a greater presence, this has not yet been the case. The second case study explores the ways in which the internet is utilised by disenfranchised social groups as a mechanism for social and collective action, and how this oppositional identity is de-legitimised. In these instances, the very tool that enables some groups to form a recognised online community is simultaneously used to disempower alternative groups seeking to find a voice.

As Benwell and Stokoe (2006: 248-9) have suggested, the emergence of a virtual community often occurs as a response by marginalised groups to oppression, and is a visible sign of resistance. One such example is the web presence for Ligali, a non-profit, voluntary organisation actively seeking to agitate for a more accurate and positive representation of African British people in the media (Ligali 2000-07). The website is suffused with issues of race, ethnicity, cultural affiliation and heritage, and provides a vivid example of identity work online. The flexibility of online communication here provides a forum within which a range of people seek support, friendship and a sense of belonging, as well as proactively pursuing and sustaining social action. As the website states, it offers an arena where more general community concerns regarding equality and exclusion are addressed, underpinned by a desire to bring about social justice. Ligali appeals for the right for self-definition and self-determination, community cohesion, freedom of speech, access and expression, equality and accountability. Importantly, Ligali attempts to narrate and recall the history of Africa and Africans *through the eyes* of Africans (Ligali 2000-07). Within the spaces created by this website, there is a focused community developing around shared interests and aspirations.

An underlying aim of the website is to provide an open record of the implicit and explicit racism often found in media and institutional responses to African British issues, as well as to document a struggle for recognition. Moreover, it is an attempt to forestall institutional, governmental and media attempts to recast history as uncontested and consensual. In this example, the entire website can be understood as a utility for creating a community forum, through its links to other organisations and movements, access to knowledge and information, and provision of an active discussion forum.

While unregistered users can observe the forum, to post and actively take part, users must read and accept a number of terms and rules that are monitored and regulated by the Ligali Team. As part of the registration process, users are asked to identify themselves in terms of whether they are African (a yes or no answer is required) and are then required to provide an indication of their cultural heritage. As physical cues for cultural and racial identities are absent online, Ligali relies on textual description. This is not confined to information provided during the registration process, as users may also take account of the social cues discernible through those perspectives revealed across a range of posts and threads. Cultural markers associated with particular cultural affiliations as found in speech are replicated in text posts, such as the reoccurrence of 'sister'/'sista'/'brother', all of which, as Burkhalter (1999) points out, are idiomatic references to African discourse.

The online community that is evidenced here is self-consciously developing around a suite of shared aims and a common purpose. Yet membership is not the same as participating in the forum, no matter how often you post. Rather, the Ligali community, like 'real life' communities, is hierarchical and heavily monitored.

> You're a member of a forum. Forum members have no say nor do they represent the views and opinions of Ligali (LP1, 2007).

> We have a very selective policy in regards to membership. We recognise that the quantity of membership is not as

important as the quality, commitment and most importantly, the collective synergy with our aims and objectives (LP2, 2007).

Nor are the exchanges that take place within the website always harmonious: indeed, at times the forum is characterised by dissent and contestation. In these instances, Ligali provides a useful illustration of interactional negotiations of identity, and an aspect of power online that is seldom acknowledged in the literature (an exception here is Burkhalter 1999). In a particularly antagonistic thread labelled *Ligali: Who Elects the Leadership – Accountability*, the cultural and racial identity of one user is explicitly challenged with the utterance:

Are you a white person? (LP3, 2007)

This post was followed by:

- Until a direct answer to this question is furnished by yourself, we will not be able to rule out the possibility of [LP4] being:
- A white supremacist racist suspect.
- 'Paleface' under the guise of an African.
- A hostage of white supremacist racists (LP3, 2007)

What this demonstrates is the power of audience reception and the online ability to re-characterise a person, in this case LP4, and their identity.

Members of Ligali appear to be motivated by reception rather than deception; an important aspect of the interaction within this space is the presentation and reception of self and identity. This we can see through attempts to replicate embodied actions usually reserved for audio-visual contexts such as the introduction of new members, or 'newbies'. Entrance into the 'settlement' is negotiated primarily through the acquisition of a username and password, but attempts to construct a serious sense of community occur through the topic 'New Members

Introduce Yourself', found in the discussion forum. This area of the website draws on the trope of 'family' and borrows from the physical world in an attempt to create a community space within which members may feel comfortable with each other among 'familiar faces' (see LP5, 2007; LP6, 2007; LP7, 2007; LP8, 2007; LP9, 2007; LP10, 2007), as the following examples illustrate:

> It is a pleasure being here and reading through the thoughts of others and interacting with the community (LP5, 2007).

> It is nice to see new people willing to learn, share and grow. I hope that we can all come together as a family to be a strong productive unit, especially in this year [2007] where we will be under constant attack from Wilberforce fans (LP11, 2007).

> … this forum is one of the few places where Africans from various backgrounds can share opinions, learn and support each other and I appreciate the work that Ligali has done and continues to do to maintain this valuable forum (LP12, 2007).

> Even if you have to just say I agree, it is nice to know that our family are always with [us] and showing support for one another (LP13, 2007).

The overarching aim of the website, however, is also of interest as it provides an oppositional voice and forum for African British people. The website and its users have been particularly active and vociferous in their opposition to official acts of commemoration surrounding the bicentenary of the abolition of the slave trade in 2007. It is with reference to expressions of dissent found within the Ligali forum that a clearer sense of the 2007 commemoration as a process of collective *forgetting* (Forty 1999: 9), or what Tunbridge and Ashworth (1996) call a process of 'disinheritance', can be discerned. Within the website, the wholly uncritical and unquestioned assumption that focussing on the 'Abolition' provides a complete, consensual and satisfactory analogue for remembering the exploitation of African people is questioned. The act of commemoration *could* have taken up a different anniversary, and certainly one in which African people are not constructed as 'passive recipients of emancipation' (Ligali 2005: 5). However, it is nonetheless the 1807 Act – which did not end the profiteering of British companies from the enslavement of African people – that came to prominence. As an online form of community, the Ligali website offers an instance within which a range of social tensions play out in what can only be described as a dynamic and complex social network. However, within this case study, it is also possible to observe the ways in which a self-identified community struggles to find legitimacy as an 'authentic' and 'trustworthy' voice *even though that voice is predominantly heard through a medium that is conventionally dismissed as either seemingly, or potentially, false*. As such, the internet offers a new venue for the development of community within the heritage sector, but it is one that also brings with it a new framework, replete with its own tensions, within which heritage professionals must negotiate with a range of interest groups about the past. Understanding and accepting the nuances of community engagement as enabled *through* the internet offers up potential advantages for heritage professionals; but they are advantages that are achievable only if we approach the medium of the internet with the same critical understandings of 'community' we are advocating for offline interactions.

Conclusion

One of the most salient observations to be made about online activity unfolding around communities is that it is a medium that has thus far failed to penetrate the full range of community groups operating in 'real life'. The current web presence

tends to be associated with professional communities or disenfranchised groups already struggling to find a legitimate and
authoritative voice. Thus, while there are many different forms
of CMC, the majority of these possibilities have not yet prolifer-
ated within the realms of heritage and archaeology. This is not
to say that there does not exist a strong presence of heritage
online. Indeed, there are a range of resources available through
online databases, podcasts and repositories. What these tend to
offer, however, is a dialogically closed interaction that is
framed by information acquisition, rather than exchange, debate and discussion. When online engagements begin to move
beyond this form of interaction, the validity and authority of
such exchanges rapidly falls away. However, the argument set
out in this chapter has revolved around an understanding of
virtual, digital and online heritage that is no longer positioned
in opposition to 'the real', and, as such, accusations that online
identities and social interactions are inauthentic, malleable
and false cease to make sense. Nor, for that matter, does the
criticism that the internet is a form of an escape from reality
hold firm. Both case studies used in this chapter tease out an
understanding of life online as something that is *real* and very
much enmeshed with the politics, social cues and cultural affiliations that animate 'real life'.

7

Conclusion: working together

We have moved through this book from the comfortable to the uncomfortable: from the proposition that policymakers and heritage professionals tend to utilise 'community' as a cosy reaffirmation of the work we do, to the idea that community interaction is contested, fraught and dissonant. Moreover, we have suggested that heritage professionals are just another community within this engagement. This dissonance is healthy, and is tied to the work heritage does as a cultural process of meaning-making. Indeed, it is a process through which those social and cultural values and narratives that help define our identities and sense of place are identified, negotiated and (re)created. As such, it is a process that will always be dissonant and conflict-ridden as it is inevitably one of inclusion and exclusion, or one that defines who belongs – and does not – in certain communities. These negotiations will have consequences for how individuals and communities are recognised or misrecognised, and will occur at both national and sub-national levels as communities define what heritage *is* and what it *means* to them.

Experts are no less engaged in these processes, though their roles are often far more formalised, and certainly authorised, through both the exercise of expertise and state heritage policy and legislation. Cultural heritage management, archaeological research and museum curation/exhibition are all processes in which meaning is made and maintained. These processes can be seen as 'heritage-making', as they are themselves creating values and narratives about the past that underpin the identities of communities of expertise. Additionally, however, and

138

unlike the narratives of many other communities, they are taken up as national narratives and often stand in for, or arbitrate on, the identities of other communities. These unequal and uneasy relations of power between communities of experts and communities of interest, together with the regulatory work that expert narratives do in any society, mean that experts will come into conflict with less powerful communities. These tensions may be quite pronounced and obvious, as expressed between Indigenous peoples and heritage professionals, or less obvious – but no less fraught – as occurs between communities operating within the same national, cultural or social contexts as experts, but whose aspirations and sense of heritage, *and what it means*, are different.

So what does this all mean for heritage professionals? For us, it requires attention to five key areas: honesty, dialogue, recognition of power, a holistic and integrated approach, and a critical regard for the political and social context of community engagement. Here, the literature on Indigenous archaeology is instructive. Primarily, this literature highlights the need for a self-aware and critical practice underpinned by clear communication, *honesty*, humility and respect (Lippert 1997; Zimmerman 2005). In this instance, honesty refers to much more than respectful and straightforward interpersonal communication. Indeed, it requires a realistic acknowledgement of what is – or is not – possible within the parameters of the project, funding and/or institutional expectations and limitations within which experts work. Further, 'honesty' also requires that heritage professionals acknowledge their own cultural, social and gendered assumptions, while also appreciating and understanding the consequences that any project may have in terms of the politics of recognition.

Dialogue thus lies at the crux of this volume, which is something that can only be developed and maintained when based on respect and an appreciation of differential power relations. Dialogically-closed 'consultation' is thus seen as problematic and is often negatively characterised as a tick-box exercise wherein experts simply 'tell' communities what is to be done.

By contrast, the idea of negotiation is central, as no consultation process can occur without a willingness to debate and accept the possibility that agendas, practices and outcomes can *and will* change. It also hinges on the development of relationships of trust, which is something that cannot be developed on promises alone, and must be earned through actions and a commitment to informed and honest ethical practice (Carter 1997; Isaacson & Ford 2005). Thus, the process of establishing and maintaining relationships, rather than simply noting their outcome, is stressed (see chapters in Swidler et al. 1997; Smith & Wobst 2005).

Another lesson derived from engagements within post-colonial contexts is that communities have knowledge and oral histories/traditions that can *and do* augment the knowledge and understanding of expert researchers and managers. That this is not always recognised tells us something about our collective inability to acknowledge that communities of expertise occupy an advantageous position of *power* over many other communities of interest, and that this has consequences for communities. In Chapter 4, we introduced the 'politics of recognition' and argued that heritage and the past become resources of power in the development of political strategies for recognition and social justice. Expertise becomes engaged not only in processes of heritage-making, but also in the arbitration and regulation of how communities are recognised or mis-recognised. An acknowledgement of this process requires communities of expertise not only to be cognisant of the consequences of the work they do, but also to self-consciously adopt political agendas. Similarly, those within community groups need to recognise the power relations they engage with, and acknowledge that experts will have the responsibility to recognise or withhold recognition according to their own ethical and political positions. Those assuming positions of representation within communities need also to realise the consequences of the internal community networks of power that they sit within, and develop honest, clear and respectful dialogues with heritage professionals. Likewise, experts must acknowledge the right that communities of interest have to refuse to work with, or abandon, communities of expertise. This may be because those communities are uninterested in, or are politically or ethically opposed to, the meanings and narratives heritage professionals have constructed or the research questions they have explored. It may also be advantageous to open dialogue with other communities of interests and share experiences, both good and bad.

That the past is political, along with the practices experts engage in to construct knowledge about it, is not a revelation. Indeed, it is a ubiquitous point within the Indigenous literature and is one that has relevance for other communities. However, the political context and cultural aspirations that underlie Indigenous power and social justice issues will *not* be the same in a European context. This is because the issues at stake for Indigenous communities arise from a history of colonial disenfranchisement and dispossession, and what we want to stress is the importance of understanding the *context* of contestation and dissonance. Thus, although we advocate the self-conscious adoption of political agendas by heritage professionals, both the context and consequences of claims need also be understood, assessed and weighed. In other words, there will be community agendas that heritage professionals will wish to support and engage with, and others that they will not. In terms of the Indigenous literature, many heritage professionals have supported the social justice claims of Indigenous peoples in recognition of the legacies of racism and discrimination of colonisation (Zimmerman 1989). Indeed, the argument, here, is that the cultural and political consequences for Indigenous peoples are such that it is vital and appropriate that they control the ways in which heritage and other cultural projects are developed, run and disseminated, and that heritage professionals engage with communities only at those communities' behest (Jackson & Smith 2005). But how should these relations of power be handled and managed outside the post-colonial context? How are such decisions made to support and recognise – or not – communities of interest? As Fraser (2001: 35) points out, not all disparities are unjust and as such:

> Claimants must show, first, that the institutionalization of majority cultural norms denies them participatory parity and, second, that the practices whose recognition they seek do not themselves deny participatory parity – to some groups members as well as to non-members.

Once again, considering the context and consequence is important in recognising certain claims and not others. How considerations of consequence and parity are weighted and assessed will invariably depend on the political agendas and moral or ethical positions that experts take.

Although the insights emerging from the literature on Indigenous engagement are useful and applicable more broadly, they are often ignored in the wider archaeological and heritage literature because they are seen as issues only relevant in cross-cultural or so-called post-colonial contexts. This tendency to compartmentalise these issues derives from the assumption that communities within one broad cultural community will understand and accept narratives about the past and heritage that *their* experts construct. Moreover, it derives from the tendency to hide any tensions that may exist under the warm and cuddly construction of community that Bauman (2001) identifies. As we have been arguing, however, these assumptions cannot be sustained. The sorts of lessons we see as transferable from the Indigenous context should not simply be reassigned into another separate or discrete context of archaeological or heritage practice, but rather *integrated into collective practice, policy and theory development*. This is because an episodic approach overlooks the wider systematic issues of social justice, recognition, status and identity that drive the creation and maintenance of community identity and use of heritage and history. Rather than ignoring the discomfort, however, the time has come for interdisciplinary and inter-community debate. Debate will need to address a range of issues. These include examining not only the roles that expert communities play in society, but also the function of the contestation between communities and expert communities and the things that this dissonance achieves. Further, the more community engagement is undertaken, the more communities of expertise will encounter – and deal with – community knowledge and experiences. Such encounters will inevitably influence and impact upon the development of archaeological and other expert knowledge. If theory and practice are indeed linked, then the interplay between this developing and central area of practice requires deeper and fuller attention. Recognising the systemic issues underlying community interactions will also illuminate the fact that heritage professionals are a community group themselves and act in much the same way as other communities to protect their interests and aspirations.

Notes

1. Heritage, communities and archaeology:
a history

1. Z. Bauman (2001) *Community: Seeking Safety in an Insecure World* (Cambridge: Polity Press), 1.

2. We opt in this volume to use CHM, although AHM is used in the UK and CRM in the US. CHM is a more inclusive term and recognises that heritage is more than archaeology. It also acknowledges that heritage should not be restricted by the term 'resource'.

3. Community dissonance

1. *Grief Tourism* can be found at
http://www.grief-tourism.com

2. *The Dark Tourism Forum* can be found at
http://www.dark-tourism.org.uk

3. Interview collected as part of the '1807 Commemorated' research project undertaken by L. Smith, G. Cubit, K. Fouseki and R. Wilson, University of York, see
http://www.history.ac.uk/1807commemorated/

4. Having a stake

1. Interview data used in this chapter is designated CCF (Cawood Craft Festival 2004), CF (Castleford Festival 2004-05) and Cas18 (Castleford oral history, interviewee number 18).

2. CCGG web address:
http://myweb.tiscali.co.uk/cawoodcastlegarth/

3. CHT web address:
http://www.castlefordheritagetrust.org.uk/

5. Museums and communities

1. Sheila Watson (2007: 2).

6. Digital communities

1. World internet usage is estimated at 1,262,032,697 people (World Stats 2007).

2. This data was gathered from www.Alexa.com, a web information company dedicated to tracking the reach of top sites per day.

3. Britarch listed 1,438 subscribers as of 24 January 2008.

Bibliography

Affleck, J. & Kvan, T. (2008) 'A virtual community as the context for discursive interpretation: a role in cultural heritage engagement', *International Journal of Heritage Studies* 14 (3), 268-80.

Agbetu, T. & Pierre, E. (2008) *The Walk: A Documentary Revealing the Truth about Pan African Resistance to Britain's 2007 Abolition and Slavery Celebrations,* DVD, Ligali Organization.

Aikawa-Faure, N. (in press 2008) 'From the proclamation of masterpieces to the convention for the safeguarding of intangible cultural heritage', in L. Smith & N. Akagawa (eds) *Intangible Heritage.* London: Routledge.

Alexander, C. (2007) 'Cohesive identities: the distance between meaning and understanding', in M. Wetherell, M. Laflèche & R. Berkeley (eds) *Identity, Ethnic Diversity and Community Cohesion,* 1115-25. London: SAGE Publications.

Alleyne, B. (2002) 'An idea of community and its discontents: towards a more reflexive sense of belonging in multicultural Britain', *Ethnic and Racial Studies* 25 (4), 607-27.

Amid, V. & Rapport, N. (2002) *The Trouble with Community: Anthropological Reflections on Movement, Identity and Collectivity.* London: Pluto Press.

Anderson, B. (1983) *Imagined Communities: Reflections on the Origin and Spread of Nationalism.* London: Verso.

Appleton, J. (2007) 'Museums for "The People"?', in S. Watson (ed.) *Museums and their Communities,* 114-26. London: Routledge.

Arantes, A.A. (2007) 'Diversity, heritage and cultural politics', *Theory, Culture and Society* 24 (7-8), 290-6.

Argyle, K. & Shields, R. (1996) 'Is there a body in the Net?', in R. Shields (ed.) *Cultures of Internet: Virtual Spaces, Real Histories, Living Bodies,* 58-69. London: SAGE Publications.

ARM (African Repartition Movement) (nd) 'Campaign for the return

of the Benin Bronzes. http://www.arm.arc.co.uk/CRBBhome.html.
Page consulted 14 July 2008.

Ashworth, G.J. (2002) 'Holocaust tourism: the experience of Krakow-Kazimierz', *International Research in Geographical and Environmental Education* 11 (4), 363-7.

———— (2008) 'The memorialization of violence and tragedy: human trauma as heritage', in B. Graham & P. Howard (eds) *The Ashgate Research Companion to Heritage and Identity*, 231-44. Aldershot: Ashgate Publishing Limited.

———— & Tunbridge, J. (1990) *The Tourist-Historic City*. New York: Wiley.

Atalay, S. (2006) 'Indigenous archaeology as decolonizing practice', *American Indian Quarterly* 30 (3&4), 280-310.

———— (2007) 'Global application of Indigenous archaeology: community based participatory research in Turkey', *Archaeologies: Journal of the World Archaeological Congress* 3 (3), 249-70.

Australian Archaeological Association (1991) *Code of Ethics*. http://www.australianarchaeologicalassociation.com.au/codeofethics.html. Page consulted 15 September 2001.

Bagnall, G. (2003) 'Performance and performativity at heritage sites', *Museum and Society* 1 (2), 87-103.

Bakardjieva, M. (2003) 'Virtual togetherness: an everyday-life perspective', *Media, Culture, Society* 25, 291-313.

Barkan, E. (2000) *The Guilt of Nations: Restitution and Negotiating Historical Injustices*. New York: W.W. Norton.

Barthel, D. (1996) *Historic Preservation: Collective Memory and Historical Identity*. New Brunswick: Rutgers University Press.

Bauman, Z. (1987) *Legislators and Interpreters*, Cambridge: Polity Press.

———— (2001) *Community: Seeking Safety in an Insecure World*. Cambridge: Polity Press.

BBC (2007) 'Discontent voiced over slavery events'. http://news.bbc.co.uk/1/hi/uk/6523327.stm. Page consulted 23 June 2008.

Beach, H. (2007) 'Self-determining the self: aspects of Saami identity management in Sweden', *Acta Borealia: A Nordic Journal of Circumpolar Societies* 24 (1), 1-25.

Beazley, O. (2007) 'A paradox of peace: the Hiroshima Peace Memorial (Genbaku Dome) as world heritage', in J. Schofield & W. Cocroft (eds) *A Fearsome Heritage: Diverse Legacies of the Cold War*, 33-50. Walnut Creek, CA: Left Coast Press.

Bell, D. (2001) *An Introduction to Cybercultures*. London: Routledge.

Bender, B. (1998) *Stonehenge: Making Space*. Oxford: Berg.

———— (2001) 'The politics of the past: Emain Macha (Navan) Northern Ireland', in R. Layton, P.G. Stone & J. Thomas (eds) *Destruction and Conservation of Cultural Property*, 199-211. London: Routledge.

Bendix, R. (in press 2008) 'Heritage between economy and politics: an assessment from the perspective of cultural anthropology', in L. Smith & N. Akagawa (eds) *Intangible Heritage*. London: Routledge.

Bennett, T. (1995) *The Birth of the Museum: History, Theory, Politics,* London: Routledge

Benwell, B. & Stokoe, E. (2006) *Discourse and Identity*. Edinburgh: Edinburgh University Press.

Betz, B. (2008) 'Putting the past to use: a plea for community archaeology', http://www.savingantiquities.org/feature_page.php?featureID=10. Page consulted 24 June 2008.

Blair, T. (2000) 'Values and the power of community', http://keeptony-blairforpm.wordpress.com/blair-speech-value-community-tubing en-30-june-2000/. Page consulted 16 May 2007.

———— (2001) 'The power of community can change the world – speech to 2001 Labour Party Conference, Brighton'. http://www.ppionline.org/ppi_ci.cfm?knlgAreaID=128&subsecID =187&contentID=3881. Page consulted 16 May 2007.

———— (2005) 'Full text: Tony Blair's speech to Faithworks'. http://politics.guardian.co.uk/speeches/story/0,,1443467,00.html. Page consulted 16 May 2007.

———— (2007) 'A message from the Prime Minister', in HM Government *2007 Bicentenary of the Abolition of the Slave Trade Act – Calendar of Events*, 1. London: Department for Communities and Local Government.

Blake, J. (in press 2008) 'UNESCO's 2003 convention on intangible cultural heritage – the implications of community involvement in "safeguarding" ', in L. Smith & N. Akagawa (eds) *Intangible Heritage*. London: Routledge.

Blanchard, A.L. & Markus, L. (2004) 'The experienced "sense" of a virtual community: characteristics and processes', *Database for Advances in Information Systems* 35 (1), 65-79.

Bona Sawa (2007) 'African Remembrance Day'. http://bonasawa.blog4ever.com/blog/lirarticle-31178-399348.html. Page consulted 30 April 2008.

149

Bibliography

Bonnell, J. & Simon, R.I. (2007) ' "Difficult" exhibitions and intimate encounters', *Museum and Society* 5 (2), 65-85.

Boyd-Barrett, O. (2004) 'Globalization, cyberspace and the public sphere', in P. Day & D. Schuler (eds) *Community Practice in the Network Society*, 23-35. London: Routledge.

Brent, J. (1997) 'Community without unity', in P. Hoggett (ed.) *Contested Communities: Experiences, Struggles, Policies*, 68-83. Bristol: Policy Press.

Brothwell, D. (2004) 'Bring out your dead: people, pots and politics', *Antiquity* 78: 414-18.

Burkhalter, B. (1999) 'Reading race online: discovering racial identity in Usenet discussions', in M.A. Smith & P. Kollock (eds) *Communities in Cyberspace*, 60-75. London: Routledge.

Byrne, D. (1991) 'Western hegemony in archaeological heritage management', *History and Anthropology* 5, 269-76.

——— (1994) 'The past of others: archaeological heritage management in Australia and Southeast Asia', unpublished PhD thesis, Australian National University.

——— (in press 2008) 'A critique of unfeeling heritage', in L. Smith & N. Akagawa (eds) *Intangible Heritage*. London: Routledge.

———, Goodall, H., Wearing, S. & Cadzow, A. (2006) 'Enchanted Parklands', *Australian Geographer* 37 (1), 103-15.

Canadian Archaeological Association (1997) 'Statement of Principles for Ethical Conduct Pertaining to Aboriginal Peoples'. http://www.canadianarchaeology.com/ethical.lasso. Page consulted 1 December 2005.

Carman, J. (1996) *Valuing Ancient Things: Archaeology and Law*. London: Leicester University Press.

——— (2001) 'Towards a 21st century archaeology for everyone: uniting current theory with the wider community', in Z. Kobyliński (ed.) *Quo Vadis Archaeologia? Whither European Archaeology in the 21st Century?*, 174-80. Warsaw: European Science Foundation & Institute of Archaeology and Ethnology of the Polish Academy of Sciences & Foundation.

——— (2002) *Archaeology and Heritage: An Introduction*. London: Continuum.

Carter, C.E. (1997) 'Straight talk and trust', in N. Swidler, K.E. Dongoske, R. Anyon & A.S. Downer (eds) *Native Americans and Archaeologists: Stepping Stones to Common Ground*, 151-5. Walnut Creek, CA: AltaMira.

Casey, D. (2007) 'Museums as agents for social and political change', in S. Watson (ed.) *Museums and their Communities*, 292-9. London: Routledge.

Cash Cash, P. (2001) 'Medicine bundles: an Indigenous approach to curation', in T. Bray (ed.) *The Future of the Past: Archaeologists, Native Americans, and Repatriation*, 139-45. New York: Garland Publishing.

CCGG (2004) Community Survey Results, unpublished report.

Chalmers, N. (2003) 'Statement of decent', in DCMS (2003) *The Report of the Working Group on Human Remains*. London: Department for Culture, Media and Sport, Cultural Property Unit.

Chivallon, C. (2001) 'Bristol and the eruption of memory: making the slave-trading past visible', *Social and Cultural Geography* 2 (3), 347-63.

Choay, F. (2001) *The Invention of the Historic Monument*. Cambridge: Cambridge University Press.

Clark, K. (2006) (ed.) *Capturing the Public Value of Heritage: The Proceedings of the London Conference 25-26 January 2006*. Swindon: English Heritage.

Clarke, A. (2002) 'The ideal and the real: cultural and personal transformations of archaeological research on Groote Eylandt, northern Australia', *World Archaeology* 34 (2), 249-64.

—— & Faulker, P. (2005) 'Living archaeology in the Madarrapa Homeland of Yilpara, north east Arnhem Land', in J. Lydon & T. Ireland (eds) *Object Lessons: Archaeology and Heritage in Australia*, 225-42. Melbourne: Australian Scholarly Publishing.

Clarke, S., Gilmore, R. & Garner, S. (2007) 'Home, identity and community cohesion', in M. Wetherell, M. Laflèche & R. Berkeley (eds) *Identity, Ethnic Diversity and Community Cohesion*, 87-101. London: SAGE Publications.

Cleere, H. (2001) 'The uneasy bedfellows: universality and cultural heritage', in R. Layton, P.G. Stone & J. Thomas (eds) *Destruction and Conservation of Cultural Property*, 22-9. London: Routledge.

Cohen, A. (1985) *The Symbolic Construction of Community*. London: Routledge.

Colwell-Chanthaphonh, C. & Ferguson, T. (2004) 'Virtue ethics and the practice of history', *Journal of Social Archaeology* 4 (1), 4-27.

Connerton, P. (1991) *How Societies Remember*. Cambridge: Cambridge University Press.

Consortium of Black Groups (COBG) (2007) 'Position statement on the bi-centenary of the abolition of the transatlantic slave trade (Maafa)'.

http://www.voscur.org/system/files/Consortium+of+Black+Groups
+statement.pdf. Page consulted 30 April 2008.

Cooper, M. (2006) 'The Pacific war battlefields: tourist attractions or
war memorials?', *International Journal of Tourism Research*, 8,
213-22.

────── (2008) 'This is not a monument: rhetorical destruction and the
social context of cultural resource management', *Public Archaeology* 7 (1), 17-30.

Crang, M. (1996) 'Living history: magic kingdoms or a quixotic quest
for authenticity?', *Annals of Tourism Research* 23 (2), 415-31.

──────, Crang, P. & May, J. (1999) 'Introduction', in M. Crang, P.
Crang & J. May (eds) *Virtual Geographies: Bodies, Space and
Relations*, 1-20. London: Routledge.

Cressey, P.J., Reeder, R. & Bryson, J. (2003) 'Held in trust: community archaeology in Alexandria, Virginia', in L. Derry & M. Malloy
(eds) *Archaeologists and Local Communities: Partners in Exploring
the Past*, 1-17. Washington, D.C.: Society for American Archaeology.

Crooke, E. (2005) 'Museums, communities and the politics of heritage
in Northern Ireland', in J. Littler & R. Naidoo (eds) *The Politics of
Heritage: The Legacies of 'Race'*, 69-81. London: Routledge.

────── (2007) *Museums and Community: Ideas, Issues and Challenges*. London: Routledge.

────── (2008) 'An exploration of the connections among museums,
community and heritage', in B. Graham & P. Howard (eds) *Ashgate
Research Companion to Heritage and Identity*, 415-24. Aldershot:
Ashgate.

Crouch, D. & Parker, G. (2003) ' "Digging-up" utopia? Space, practice
and landuse heritage', *Geoforum* 34, 395-408.

Crow, G. & Allen, G. (1994) *Community Life: An Introduction to Local
Social Relations*. London: Harvester Wheatsheaf.

Davis, P. (1999) *Ecomuseums: A Sense of Place*. London: Leicester
University Press.

────── (2007) 'Place exploration: museums, identity, community', in S.
Watson (ed.) *Museums and their Communities*, 53-75. London:
Routledge.

Day, G. & Murdoch, J. (1993) 'Locality and community: coming to
terms with places', *Sociological Review* 41 (1), 82-111.

DCMS (2001) 'The historic environment: a force for our future'.
www.culture.gov.uk/global/publications/archive_2001/his_force_
future.htm. Page consulted 3 July 2003.

Bibliography

—— (2002) 'People and places: social inclusion policy for the built and historic environment'. http://www.culture.gov.uk/NR/ rdonlyres/ejeviot6kt5wvcz2osn5dbafmfunonotnqasogvrmbsjj3tyu uhyxvmmsopvcbmvehgqiwsz4cfta7e6jhhjnfbhqxh/people_and_pl aces.pdf. Page consulted 5 April 2004.

—— (2003) *The Report of the Working Group on Human Remains.* London: Department for Culture, Media and Sport, Cultural Property Unit.

—— (2007) 'Taking part: the national survey of culture, leisure and sport, annual report 2005/2006'. http://www.culture.gov.uk/ Reference_library/Research/taking_part_survey/surveyoutputs_ may07.htm. Page consulted 7 June 2007.

Deloria, V. Jr. (1992) 'Indians, archaeologists, and the future', *American Antiquity* 57(4), 595-8.

Diaz-Andreu, M. (2007) *A World History of Nineteenth-Century Archaeology. Nationalism, Colonialism, and the Past.* Oxford: Oxford University Press.

Dickenson, V. (2006) 'History, ethnicity and citizenship: the role of the history museum in a multi-ethnic country', *Museum International* 58 (3), 21-31.

Dicks, B. (2000a) *Heritage, Place and Community.* Cardiff: University of Wales Press.

—— (2000b) 'Encoding and decoding the people: circuits of communication at a local heritage museum', *European Journal of Communication* 15 (1), 61-78.

—— (2003) *Culture on Display: The Production of Contemporary Visitability.* Maidenhead: Open University Press.

—— (2008) 'Performing the hidden injuries of class in coal-mining heritage', *Sociology* 43(3), 436-52.

Dodd, J. & Sandell, R. (2001) *Including Museums: Perspectives on Museums, Galleries and Social Inclusion.* Leicester: Research Centre for Museums and Galleries.

——, Sandell, R., Delin, A. & Gay, J. (2004) 'Buried in the footnotes: the representation of disabled people in museum and gallery collections', http://www.le.ac.uk/museumstudies/research/Reports/BITF2.pdf. Page consulted 12 July 2008.

Donath, J.S. (1999) 'Identity and deception in the virtual community', in M.A. Smith & P. Kollock (eds) *Communities in Cyberspace*, 29-59. London: Routledge.

Downer, A.S. (1997) 'Archaeologists-Native American relations', in N. Swidler, K.E. Dongoske, R. Anyon & A.S. Downer (eds) *Native*

Americans and Archaeologists: Stepping Stones to Common Ground, 23-34. Walnut Creek, CA: AltaMira.

Drake, A. (2004) The Castleford Heritage Project: A Personal View. Paper presented at the Heritage Lottery Fund Conference, Dublin, Ireland.

———— (2008) 'The use of community heritage in pursuit of social inclusion: a case study of Castleford, West Yorkshire', unpublished Masters dissertation, University of York.

Dresser, M. (2007) *Slavery Obscured: The Social History of the Slave Trade in Bristol*, Redcliffe Press.

Ellemor, H. (2003) 'White skin, black heart? The politics of belonging and Native Title in Australia', *Social and Cultural Geography* 4 (2), 233-52.

Englestad, E. (1991) 'Images of power and contradiction: feminist theory and post-processual archaeology', *Antiquity* 65, 502-14.

English Heritage (2000a) 'Power of place: the future of the historic environment'. http://www.english-heritage.org.uk/filestore/policy/government/mori/finalreport/11.pdf. Page consulted 3 July 2003.

———— (2000b) *First Draft of Discussion Paper for WG1.*

———— (2005a) *Discovering the Past, Shaping the Future: Research Strategy 2005-2010.* http://www.english-heritage.org.uk/upload/pdf/Research_Strategy .pdf. Page consulted 23 June 2008.

———— (2005b) *English Heritage Strategy 2005-2010: Making the Past Part of our Future.* Swindon: English Heritage.

———— (2005c) Principles for the sustainable management of the historic environment – Draft 02, unpublished document.

———— (2006a) *Heritage Counts: The State of England's Historic Environment 2006.* London: English Heritage.

———— (2006b) *Conservation Principles for the Sustainable Management of the Historic Environment.* London: English Heritage.

Englund, H. (2004) 'Introduction: recognizing identities, imagining alternatives', in H. Englund & F.B. Nyamnjoh (eds) *Rights and the Politics of Recognition in Africa*, 1-29. London: Zed Books.

Evans & Harris (2004) 'Citizenship, social inclusion and confidentiality', *British Journal of Social Work* 34(1), 69-91.

Facebook (2007) 'Statistics'. http://www.facebook.com/press/info.php?statistics. Page consulted 14 January 2008.

Fairclough, N. (2000) *New Labour, New Language?* London: Routledge.

Falch, T. & Skandfer, M. (2004) 'Sámi cultural heritage in Norway: between local knowledge and the power of the state', in I. Krupnik, R. Mason & T. Horton (eds) *Northern Ethnographic Landscapes: Perspectives from Circumpolar Nations*, 356-75. Washington DC: Smithsonian Institute.

Falk, J.H. & Dierking, D.L. (2000) *Learning from Museums: Visitor Experiences and the Making of Meaning*. Walnut Creek, CA: AltaMira.

Fforde, C., Hurbert, J. & Turnball, P. (2002) (eds) *The Dead and their Possessions: Repatriation in Principle, Policy and Practice*. London: Routledge.

Forty, A. (1999) 'Introduction', in A. Forty & S. Külcher (eds) *The Art of Forgetting*, 1-18. Oxford: Berg.

Fouseki, K. (2008) 'Community consultation as mediation of a contentious past', paper presented at the World Archaeological Congress 6, July, Dublin, Ireland.

Fraser, N. (1999) 'Social justice in the age of identity politics: redistribution, recognition, and participation', in L. Ray & A. Sayer (eds) *Culture and Economy After the Cultural Turn*, 25-52. London: SAGE Pubications.

—— (2000) 'Rethinking recognition', *New Left Review* 3 (May/June), 107-20.

—— (2001) 'Recognition without ethics?', *Theory, Culture and Society* 18 (2-3), 21-42.

Fyfe, G. (1996) 'A Trojan Horse at the Tate: theorizing the museum as agency and structure', in S. Macdonald & G. Fyfe (eds) *Theorizing Museums*, 203-28. Oxford: Blackwell.

—— & Ross, M. (1996) 'Decoding the visitor's gaze: rethinking museum visiting', in S. Macdonald & G. Fyfe (eds) *Theorizing Museums*, 125-50. Oxford: Blackwell.

Gabriel, D. (2007) 'International day for the remembrance of slavery must be about action not nostalgia'. http://www.iamcolourful.com/articles/Comment/details/2144318321/World/. Page consulted 6 May 2008.

Geurds, A. (2007) *Grounding the Past: The Praxis of Participatory Archaeology in the Mixteca Alta, Oaxaca, Mexico*. Leiden: CNWS Publications.

Gieryn, T.F. (1998) 'Balancing acts: science, Enola Gay and the history wars at the Smithsonian', in S. MacDonald (ed.) *The Politics of Display: Museums, Science, Culture*, 197-228. London: Routledge.

Graham, B. (1998) 'Contested images of place among Protestants in Northern Ireland', *Political Geography* 17 (2), 129-44.

———— & Shirlow, P. (2002) 'The Battle of the Somme in Ulster memory and identity', *Political Geography* 21, 881-904.

————, Ashworth, G. & Tunbridge, J. (2000) *A Geography of Heritage: Power, Culture and Economy*. London: Arnold Publishers.

Green, C. (1996) 'Helping to make it happen', *Conservation Bulletin* 28, 1.

Green, L.F., Green, D.R. & Goes Neves, E. (2003) 'Indigenous knowledge and archaeological science', *Journal of Social Archaeology* 3 (3), 366-98.

Greer, S., Harrison, R. & McIntyre-Tamwoy, S. (2002) 'Community-based archaeology in Australia', *World Archaeology* 34 (2), 265-87.

Grossman, L. (2006) 'Time's person of the year: You', *TIME Magazine* 168 (26), 1-3.

Hall, S. (1999) 'Whose heritage? Un-settling "the heritage", re-imagining the post-nation', *Third Text* 49, 3-13.

Hamilakis, Y. (1999) 'Stories from exile: fragments from cultural biography of the Parthenon (or 'Elgin') marbles', *World Archaeology* 31(2), 303-20

Handler, R. & Gable, E. (1997) *The New History in an Old Museum: Creating the Past at Colonial Williamsburg*. Durham, NC: Duke University Press.

Harvey, D.C. (2001) 'Heritage pasts and heritage presents: temporality, meaning and the scope of heritage studies', *International Journal of Heritage Studies* 7 (4), 319-38.

Hesse, B. (2002) 'Forgotten like a bad dream: Atlantic slavery and ethics of postcolonial memory', in D.T. Goldberg & A. Quayson (eds) *Relocating Postcolonialism*, 143-73. Oxford: Blackwell.

Hewison, R. (1987) *The Heritage Industry: Britain in a Climate of Decline*. London: Meltuen London Ltd.

Ho, S. (2007) 'Blogging as popular history making: blogs as public history', *Public History Review* 14, 64-79.

Hodder, I. (1996) *On the Surface: Catalhöyük 1993-1995*. Cambridge: McDonald Institute Monographs.

———— (2002) 'Ethics and archaeology: the attempt at Catalhoyuk', *Near Eastern Archaeology* 65 (3), 174-81.

———— (2003) 'Social thought and commentary: archaeological reflexivity and the "local" voice', *Anthropological Quarterly* 79 (1), 55-69.

Bibliography

Hodge, M. (2008) 'Margaret Hodge's speech on Britishness, heritage and the Arts', IPPR event, National Portrait Gallery, Department for Culture Media and Sport'. http://www.culture.gov.uk/reference_library/minister_speeches/2002.aspx. Page consulted 13 May 2008.

Hodges, A. & Watson, S. (2000) 'Community-based heritage management: a case study and agenda for research', *International Journal of Heritage Studies* 6 (3), 231-43.

Hoggett, P. (1997) 'Contested communities', in P. Hoggett (ed.) *Contested Communities: Experiences, Struggles, Policies*, 3-16. Bristol: Policy Press.

Hoobler, E. (2006) '"To take their heritage in their hands": Indigenous self-representation and decolonization in the community museums of Oaxaca, Mexico', *American Indian Quarterly* 30 (3/4), 441-62.

Hooper-Greenhill, E. (2007) *Museums and Education: Purpose, Pedagogy, Performance*. London: Routledge.

Hubbard, B. & Hasian, M.A. (1998) 'The genetic roots of the *Enola Gay* controversy', *Political Communication* 4(1), 497-513.

Hudson, K. (2004) 'Behind the rhetoric of community development: how is it perceived and practiced?', *Australian Journal of Social Issues* 39 (3), 249-65.

Huyssen, A. (1995) *Twilight Memories: Marking Time in a Culture of Amnesia*. London: Routledge.

Isaacson, K. & Ford, S. (2005) 'Looking forward – looking back: shaping a shared future', in C. Smith & H.M. Wobst (eds) *Indigenous Archaeologies: Decolonizing Theory and Practice*, 354-67. London: Routledge.

Jackson, G. & Smith, C. (2005) 'Living and learning on Aboriginal lands: decolonizing archaeology in practice', in C. Smith & H.M. Wobst (eds) *Indigenous Archaeologies: Decolonizing Theory and Practice*, 328-51. London: Routledge.

Jarman, N. (1999) 'Commemorating 1916, celebrating difference: parading and painting in Belfast', in A. Forty & S. Kuchler (eds) *The Art of Forgetting*, 171-95. Oxford: Berg.

Jenkins, T. 2003 'Burying the evidence', *Spiked Culture*, 24 November. http://www.spiked-online.com/Articles. Page consulted 12 January 2004.

Jones, S. (2004) *Early Medieval Sculpture and the Production of Meaning, Value and Place: The Case of Hilton of Cadboll*. Edinburgh: Historic Scotland.

——— (2005) 'Making place, resisting displacement: conflicting national and local identities in Scotland', in J. Littler & R. Naidoo

157

(eds) *The Politics of Heritage: The Legacies of 'Race'*, 94-114. London: Routledge.

———— (2006) ' "They made it a living thing didn't they ... " The growth of things and the fossilization of heritage', in R. Layton, S. Shennan & P. Stone (eds) *A Future for Archaeology: The Past in the Present*, 107-26. London: Cavendish Publishing.

Jones, S.G. (1997) 'The Internet and its social landscape', in S.G. Jones (ed.) *Virtual Culture: Identity and Communication in Cyberspace*, 7-35. London: SAGE Publications.

Joseph, J. & Roberts, J.M. (2004) 'Introduction: realism, discourse and deconstruction', in J. Joseph & J.M. Roberts (eds) *Realism Discourse and Deconstruction*, 1-19. London: Routledge.

Katriel, T. (1994) 'Sites of memory – discourses of the past in Israeli Pioneering Settlement Museums', *Quarterly Journal of Speech* 80 (1), 1-20.

Karp, I. (1992) 'On civil society and social identity', in I. Karp, C.M. Kreamer & S.D. Kavube (eds) *Museums and Communities: The Politics of Public Culture*, 19-33. Washington DC: Smithsonian.

Kavanaugh, A. (1999) 'The impact of computer networking on community: a social network analysis approach', paper presented at the Telecommunications Policy Research Conference, September 27-29, 1999. http://www.ntia.doc.gov/top/research/reports/tprc.userstudy.kavanaugh.pdf. Page consulted 16 January 2008.

Kawashima, N. (2006) 'Audience development and social inclusion in Britain: tensions, contradictions and paradoxes in policy and their implications for cultural management', *International Journal of Cultural Property* 12 (1), 55-72.

Kelly, L. (2004) 'Evaluation, research and communities of practice: program evaluation in museums', *Archival Science* 4, 45-69.

———— & Gordon, P. (2002) 'Developing a community of practice: museums and reconciliation in Australia', in R. Sandell (ed.) *Museums, Society, Inequality*, 153-74. London: Routledge.

Kirshenblatt-Gimblett, B. (1998) *Destination Culture: Tourism, Museums and Heritage*, Berkeley, CA: University of California Press.

Kishimoto, K. (2004) 'Apologies for atrocities: commemorating the 50th anniversary of World War II's end in the United States and Japan', *American Studies International* 42 (2/3), 17-50.

Koller, V. & Davidson, P. (2008) 'Social exclusion as conceptual and grammatical metaphor: a cross-genre study of British policymaking', *Discourse and Society* 19 (3), 307-31.

Bibliography

Kollock, P. & Smith, M. (1996) 'Managing the virtual commons: cooperation and conflict in computer communities', in S. Herring (ed.) *Computer-Mediated Communication: Linguistic, Social and Cross-Cultural Perspectives*, 109-28. Amsterdam: John Benjamins.

Kumar, C. (2005) 'Revisiting "community" in community-based natural resource management', *Community Development Journal* 40 (3), 275-85.

Kurin, R. (2004) 'Safeguarding intangible cultural heritage in the 2003 UNESCO Convention: a critical appraisal', *Museum International* 56 (1-2), 66-77.

Kymlicka, W. & Norman, W. (2000) 'Citizenship in culturally diverse societies: issues, contexts, concepts', in W. Kymlicka & W. Norman (eds) *Citizenship in Diverse Societies*, 1-41. Oxford: Oxford University Press.

Labadi, S. (2007) 'Representations of the nation and cultural diversity in discourses on World Heritage', *Journal of Social Archaeology* 7 (2), 147-70.

Lahn, J. (1996) 'Finders keepers, losers weepers: a "social history" of the Kow Swamp remains', *Ngulaig* 15, 1-61.

Langford, R. (1983) 'Our heritage – your playground', *Australian Archaeology* 16, 1-6.

Leone, M.P., Potter, P.B. Jr. & Shackel, P.A. (1987) 'Toward a critical archaeology', *Current Anthropology* 28(3), 283-302

Levitas, R. (2005) *The Inclusive Society? Social Exclusion and New Labour*. Hampshire: Palgrave Macmillan.

Levy, D. & Sznaider, N. (2002) 'Memory unbound: the holocaust and the formation of cosmopolitan memory', *European Journal of Social Theory* 5 (1), 87-106.

Liddle, P. (1985) *Community Archaeology: A Fieldworkers Handbook of Organisation and Techniques*. Leicester: Leicester Museums, Art Galleries and Records Service.

Ligali (2000-07) 'Ligali – Equality for African people'. http://www.ligali.org/index.php. Page consulted 8 October 2007.

—— (2005) 'Declaration of protest to the 2007 commemoration of the bicentenary of the British parliamentary abolition of the transatlantic slave trade'. London: The Ligali Organisation. http://www.africanholocaust.net/articles/Declaration%20of%20protest%20to%20the%202007%20Abolition%20Commemoration.pdf. Page consulted 23 June 2008.

Linkon, S.L. & Russo, J. (2002) *Steeltown U.S.A.: Work and Memory in Youngstown*. Lawrence: University of Press of Kansas.

Bibliography

Lippert, D. (1997) 'In front of the mirror: Native Americans and academic archaeology', in N. Swidler, K.E. Dongoske, R. Anyon & A.S. Downer (eds) *Native Americans and Archaeologists: Stepping Stones to Common Ground*, 120-7. Walnut Creek, CA: AltaMira.

Littler, J. & Naidoo, R. (2004) 'White past, multicultural present: heritage and national stories', in H. Brocklehurst & R. Phillips (eds) *History, Nationhood and the Question of Britain*, 330-41. Basingstoke: Palgrave Macmillan.

—— (eds) (2005) *The Politics of Heritage: The Legacies of 'Race'*. London: Routledge.

Logan, W. & Reeves, K. (eds) (in press) *Places of Pain and Shame: Dealing with 'Difficult' Heritage*. London: Routledge.

Longhurst, B., Bagnall, G. & Savage, M. (2004) 'Audiences, museums and the English middle class', *Museum and Society* 2 (2), 104-24.

Lynott, M. & Wylie, A. (eds) (2000) *Ethics in American Archaeology*. Washington DC: Society for American Archaeology.

McClanahan, A. (2007) 'The cult of community: defining the "local" in public archaeology and heritage discourse', in S. Grabow, D. Hull & E. Waterton (eds) *Which Past, Whose Future? The Past at the Start of the 21st Century*, 51-7. Oxford: Archaeopress.

McDavid, C. (2004) 'From "traditional" archaeology to public archaeology to community action', in P.A. Shackel & E.J. Chambers (eds) *Places in Mind: Public Archaeology as Applied Anthropology*, 35-56. New York: Routledge.

Macdonald, S. (1998) 'Exhibitions of power and powers of exhibitions: an introduction to the politics of display', in S. Macdonald (ed.) *The Politics of Display: Museums, Science, Culture,* 1-24. London: Routledge.

—— (2002) 'On "old things": the fetishization of past everyday life', in Nigel Rapport (ed.) *British Subjects: An Anthropology of Britain*, 89-106. Oxford: Berg.

—— (2003) 'Museums, national, postnational and transcultural identities', *Museum and Society* 1 (1), 1-16.

—— (2005) 'Commemorating the Holocaust: reconfiguring national identity in the twenty-first century', in J. Littler & R. Naidoo (eds) *The Politics of Heritage: The Legacies of 'Race'*, 49-68. London: Routledge.

—— (2006a) 'Undesirable heritage: fascist material culture and historical consciousness in Nuremberg', *International Journal of Heritage Studies* 12 (1), 9-28.

Bibliography

——— (2006b) 'Mediating heritage: tour guides at the former Nazi Party rally grounds, Nuremberg', *Tourist Studies* 6(2), 119-38.

McGimsey, C.R. (1972) *Public Archaeology*. New York: Seminar Press.

MacGregor, S. (2001) 'The problematic community', in M. May, R. Page & E. Brunsdon (eds) *Understanding Social Problems: Issues in Social Policy*, 187-204. Oxford: Blackwell.

McNiven, I. & Russell, L. (eds) (2005) *Appropriated Pasts: Indigenous Peoples and the Colonial Culture of Archaeology*. Walnut Creek, CA: AltaMira.

Malloy, M. (2003) 'Introduction', in L. Derry & M. Malloy (eds) *Archaeologists and Local Communities: Partners in Exploring the Past*, ix-xiii. Washington, DC: Society for American Archaeology.

Mandler, P. (1997) *The Fall and Rise of the Stately Home*. New Haven: Yale University Press.

Markham, A.N. (1998) *Life Online: Researching Real Experience in Virtual Space*. Walnut Creek, CA: AltaMira.

Marquis-Kyle, P. & Walker, M. (1992) (eds) *The Illustrated Burra Charter: Making Good Decisions about the Care of Important Places*. Sydney: Australia ICOMOS.

Marshall, Y. (2002) 'What is community archaeology?' *World Archaeology* 34 (2), 211-19.

Mason, R. (2005) 'Museums, galleries and heritage: sites of meaning-making and communication', in G. Corsane (ed.) *Heritage, Museums and Galleries: An Introductory Reader*, 200-14. London: Routledge.

Merriman, N. (1989) 'Museum visiting as a cultural phenomenon', in P. Vergo (ed.) *The New Museology*, 149-71. London: Reaktion Books.

——— (2002) 'Archaeology, heritage and interpretation', in B. Cunliffe, W. Davies & C. Renfrew (eds) *Archaeology: The Widening Debate*, 541-66. Oxford: Oxford University Press.

——— (2004) 'Introduction: diversity and dissonance in public archaeology', in N. Merriman (ed.) *Public Archaeology*, 1-17. London: Routledge.

Meskell, L. (2005) 'Deconstructing gender in prehistory', in S. McKinnon & S. Silverman (eds) *Complexities: Beyond Nature and Nurture*, 157-75. Chicago: University of Chicago Press.

Miller, J. (1986) *Koori: A Will to Win*. North Ryde: Angus & Robertson.

Misztal, B. (2003) *Theories of Social Remembering*. Milton Keynes: Open University Press.

Mitchell, S. (1999) Hareshaw Oral History Community Project: Report and Recommendations, unpublished report.

Bibliography

Molz, J.G. (2004) 'Playing online and between the lines: round-the-world websites as virtual places to play', in M. Sheller & J. Urry (eds) *Tourism Mobilities: Places to Play, Places in Play*, 169-80. London: Routledge.

Morris, W. (1877) *Manifesto of the Society for the Protection of Ancient Buildings*. London: Society for the Protection of Ancient Buildings.

Moser, S., Glazier, D., Phillips, J.E., Nasser el Nemr, L., Mousa, M.S., Aiesh, R.N., Richardson, S., Connor, A. & Seymore, M. (2002) 'Transforming archaeology through practice: strategies for collaborative archaeology and the Community Archaeology Project at Quseir, Egypt', *World Archaeology* 34 (2), 220-48.

Müller, D.K. & Pettersson, R. (2001) 'Access to Sami Tourism in Northern Sweden', *Scandinavian Journal of Hospitality and Tourism* 1 (1), 5-18.

Museums Australia (1999) 'Policies: continuous cultures, ongoing responsibilities'. http://www.museumsaustralia.org.au/structure/policies/ppno/ccor.htm. Page consulted 22 March 2004.

My Space (2007) 'About us', http://www.myspace.com/index.cfm?fuseaction=misc.aboutus. Page consulted 14 January 2008.

Nakamura, L. (2000) 'Race in/for cyberspace: identity tourism and racial passing on the Internet', in D. Bell & B.M. Kennedy (eds) *The Cyberspace Reader*, 712-20. London: Routledge.

Nalda, E. (2005) 'Mexican archaeology and its inclusion in the debate on diversity and identity', *Museum International* 57 (3), 32-43.

Neal, S. & Walters, S. (2008) 'Rural be/longing and rural social organizations: conviviality and community-making in the English countryside', *Sociology* 42(2), 279-97.

NetRatings (2006) 'Social networking sites grow 47 percent, year over year, reaching 45 percent of web users, according to Nielson/Netratings'. http://www.nielsen-netratings.com/pr/pr_060511.pdf. Page consulted 12 January 2008.

Newman, A. & McLean, F. (2006) 'The impact of museums upon identity', *International Journal of Heritage Studies* 12 (1), 49-68.

Nicholas, G.P. & Hollowell, J. (2007) 'Ethical challenges to a postcolonial archaeology: the legacy of scientific colonialism', in Y. Hamilakas & P. Duke (eds) *Archaeology and Capitalism: From Ethics to Politics*, 59-82. London: University College London.

Nora, P. (1989) 'Between memory and history: *Les Lieux de Memoire*', *Representations* 26 (Spring), 7-24.

Northumberland National Park (1999) 'The Hareshaw Linn Project', *News*. Hexham: NNPA.

Bibliography

Novick, P. (1999) *The Holocaust and Collective Memory: The American Experience*. London: Bloomsbury.

Oliver, B. & Reeves, A. (2003) 'Crossing disciplinary boundaries: labour history and museum studies', *Labour History*. http:www.historycooperative.org/journals/lab/85/oliver.html. Page consulted 1 August 2005.

Operation Truth (2007) 'Homepage – Operation Truth 2007'. http://www.operationtruth2007.co.uk/index.htm. Page consulted 23 June 2008.

Orr, T. (2004) 'The information-seeking behaviour of museum visitors: a review of literature'. http://home.earthlink.net/~toriorr/ROL_MuseumVisitors.doc. Page consulted 19 June 2008.

Pearson, M. & Sullivan, S. (1995) *Looking after Heritage Places: The Basics of Heritage Planning for Managers, Landowners and Administrators*. Melbourne: Melbourne University Press.

Pevsner, N. ([1959] 1986) *The Buildings of England: Yorkshire: The West Riding,* Harmondsworth: Penguin.

Phillips, A. (1995) *The Politics of Presence: The Political Representation of Gender, Ethnicity, and Race*. Oxford: Oxford University Press.

Pietroni, E. & Forte, M. (2007) 'A virtual collaborative environment for archaeology through multi-user domain in the web'. http://cipa.icomos.org/fileadmin/papers/Athens2007/FP116.pdf. Page consulted 23 January 2008.

Poria, Y., Butler, R. & Airey, D. (2003) 'The core of heritage tourism', *Annals of Tourism Research* 30 (1), 238-54.

Porter, G. (1996), 'Seeing through solidity: a feminist perspective on museums', in S. Macdonald & G. Fyfe (eds) *Theorising Museums,* 105-26. Oxford: Blackwell.

Porter, L. (2004) 'Unlearning one's privilege: reflections on cross-cultural research with Indigenous peoples in South-East Australia', *Planning Theory & Practice* 5 (1), 104-9.

——— (2006) 'Rights or containment? The politics of Aboriginal cultural heritage in Victoria', *Australian Geographer* 37 (3), 355-74.

Rheingold, H. (1993) *The Virtual Community: Homesteading on the Electronic Frontier*. Reading, MA: Addison-Wesley.

Richardson, J.E. (2007) *Analysing Newspapers: An Approach from Critical Discourse Analysis*. Basingstoke: Palgrave Macmillan.

Riley, M. & Harvey, D. (2005) 'Landscape archaeology, heritage and the community in Devon: an oral history approach', *International Journal of Heritage Studies* 11 (4), 269-88.

Ross, M. (2004) 'Interpreting the new museology', *Museum and Society* 2 (2), 84-103.

Rountree, K. (2007) 'Archaeologists and Goddess feminists at Catalhoyuk', *Journal of Feminist Studies in Religion* 23 (3), 7-26.

Ruskin, J. (1849) *The Seven Lamps of Architecture*. London: Smith.

Samuel, R. (1994) *Theatres of Memory*, vol. 1: *Past and Present in Contemporary Culture*. London: Verso.

Sandell, R. (2002) 'Museums and the combating of social inequality: roles, responsibilities, resistance', in R. Sandell (ed.) *Museums, Society, Inequality*, 3-23. London: Routledge.

—— (2003) 'Social inclusion, the museum and the dynamics of sectorial change', *Museum and Society* 1 (1), 45-62.

—— (2007) *Museums, Prejudice and the Reframing of Difference*. London: Routledge.

Savage, M., Bagnall, G. & Longhurst, B. (2005) *Globalisation and Belonging*. London: SAGE Publications.

Sculthorpe, G. (2005) 'Recognizing difference: contested issues in Native Title and cultural heritage', *Anthropological Forum* 15 (2), 171-93.

Seaton, A.V. (1999) 'War and thanatourism: Waterloo 1815-1914', *Annals of Tourism Research* 26 (1), 130-58.

Selwood, S. (2006) 'Unreliable evidence: the rhetoric of data collection in the cultural sector', in M. Mirza (ed.) *Culture Vultures: Is UK Arts Policy Damaging the Arts,* 38-53. London: Policy Exchange.

Sen, S. (2002) 'Community boundary, secularized religion and imagined past in Bangladesh: archaeology and historiography of unequal encounter', *World Archaeology* 34 (2), 346-62.

Shandler, J. (1999) 'Heritage and the holocaust on display: New York City's Museum of Jewish Heritage – a living memorial to the Holocaust', *Public Historian* 21 (1), 73-86.

Sharpe, B. (1998) ' "First the forest": conservation, "community" and "participation" in South-West Cameroon', *Africa: Journal of the International African Institute* 68 (1), 25-45.

Shepherd, N. (2003) 'State of the discipline: science, culture and identity in South African archaeology', *Journal of Southern African Studies*, 29 (4), 823-44.

Siegenthaler, P. (2002) 'Hiroshima and Nagasaki in Japanese guidebooks', *Annals of Tourism Research* 29 (4), 1111-37.

Simon, R.I. (2006) 'The terrible gift: museums and the possibility of hope without consolation', *Museum Management and Curatorship* 21 (3), 187-204.

Simpson, M. (2007) 'From treasure house to museum … and back', in S. Watson (ed.) *Museums and their Communities*. London: Routledge.

Skeates, R. (2000) *Debating the Archaeological Heritage*. London: Duckworth.

Smith, C. & Jackson, G. (2006) 'Decolonizing Indigenous archaeology: developments from Down Under', *American Indian Quarterly* 30 (3 & 4), 311-49.

—— & Wobst, H.M. (eds) (2005) *Indigenous Archaeologies: Decolonising Theory and Practice*. London: Routledge.

Smith, L. (1994) 'Heritage management as postprocessual archaeology?', *Antiquity* 68, 300-9.

—— (2000) ' "Doing archaeology": cultural heritage management and its role in identifying the link between archaeological practice and theory', *International Journal of Heritage Studies* 6 (4), 309-16.

—— (2004a) *Archaeological Theory and the Politics of Cultural Heritage*. London: Routledge.

—— (2004b) 'The repatriation of human remains – problem or opportunity', *Antiquity* 78: 404-13.

—— (2006) *The Uses of Heritage*. London: Routledge.

—— (2007) 'General introduction', in L. Smith (ed.) *Cultural Heritage: Critical Concepts in Media and Cultural Studies*, vol. 1, 1-21. London: Routledge.

—— (2008a) 'Heritage, gender and identity', in B. Graham & P. Howard (eds) *Ashgate Research Companion to Heritage and Identity*. Aldershot: Ashgate.

—— (2008b) ' "Man's inhumanity to man" and other platitudes of avoidance and misrecognition'. Paper presented at the World Archaeological Congress 6, July 2008, Dublin, Ireland.

—— & Waterton, E. (in press 2008) ' "The envy of the world?": intangible heritage in England', in L. Smith & N. Akagawa (eds) *Intangible Heritage*. London: Routledge.

Stacey, M. (1969) 'The myth of community studies', *British Journal of Sociology* 20 (2), 134-47.

Strangleman, T. (1999) 'The nostalgia of organisations and the organisation of nostalgia: past and present in the contemporary railway industry', *Sociology* 33 (4), 725-46.

Swain, H. (2007) *An Introduction to Museum Archaeology*. Cambridge: Cambridge University Press.

Swidler, N., Dongoske, K.E., Anyon, R. & Downer, A.S. (eds) (1997) *Native Americans and Archaeologists: Stepping Stones to Common Ground*. Walnut Creek, CA: AltaMira.

165

Szekeres, V. (2002) 'Representing diversity and challenging racism: the Migration Museum', in R. Sandell (ed.) *Museums and their Communities*, 142-52. London: Routledge.

Teye, V.B. & Timothy, D.J. (2004) 'The varied colors of slave heritage in West Africa: white American stakeholders', *Space and Culture* 7, 145-55.

Thompson, B. & Thompson, P. (1999) Transcript of Oral History Recording, recorded by S. Mitchell on 20 July 1999, as part of the Hareshaw Linn Community Project, archive tape number HOH/19, held at the Northumberland National Park Headquarters.

Thrift, N. (2005) 'But malice aforethought: cities and the natural history of hatred', *Transaction of the Institute of British Geographers* 30 (2), 133-50.

Tlili, A. (2008) 'Behind the policy mantra of the inclusive museum: receptions of social exclusion and inclusion in museums and science centres', *Cultural Sociology* 2 (1), 123-47.

Trigger, B. (1995) 'Romanticism, nationalism and archaeology', in P.L. Kohl & C. Fawcett (eds) *Nationalism, Politics and the Practice of Archaeology*, 263-79. Cambridge: Cambridge University Press.

Tully, G. (2007) 'Community archaeology: general methods and standards of practice', *Public Archaeology* 6 (3), 155-87.

Tunbridge, J.E. & Ashworth, G. (1996) *Dissonant Heritage: The Management of the Past as a Resource in Conflict*. Chichester: Wiley.

Urry, J. (1996) 'How societies remember the past', in S. Macdonald & G. Fyfe (eds) *Theorising Museums*, 45-65. Oxford: Blackwell.

Vanden Berghe, K. & Maddens, B. (2004) 'Ethnocentrism, nationalism and post-nationalism in the tales of Subcomandante Marcos', *Mexican Studies* 20 (1), 123-44.

Vergo, P. (ed.) (1989) *The New Museology*, London: Reaktion Books.

Viollet-le-Duc, E. ([1868] 1990) *The Foundations of Architecture: Selections from the Dictionnaire Raisonné*; reprint trans. D. Whitehead. NY: Braziller.

Walker, T. (1984) 'Guardians of community heritage', *Municipal Journal* 92, 1981-82.

Wallace, M. (1996) *Mickey Mouse History and Other Essays on American Memory*. Philadelphia: Temple University Press.

Waterton, E. (2005) 'Whose sense of place? Reconciling archaeological perspectives with community values: cultural landscapes in England', *International Journal of Heritage Studies* 11 (4), 309-26.

——— (2007a) 'Rhetoric and "reality": politics, policy and the discourses of heritage in England', unpublished PhD thesis, University of York.

—— (2007b) 'An institutionalised construction of the past in the UK', in D. Hull, S. Grabow & E. Waterton (eds) *Which Past, Whose Future? Treatments of the Past at the Start of the 21st Century*, 31-9. Oxford: Archaeopress.

—— (2008a, in press) 'Sites of sights: picturing power, heritage and exclusion', *Journal of Heritage Tourism*.

—— (2008b, in press) 'Invisible identities: destroying the heritage of Cawood Castle', in L. Rakoczy (ed.) *An Archaeology of Destruction*. Cambridge: Scholars Press.

——, Smith, L. & Campbell, G. (2006) 'The utility of discourse analysis to heritage studies: the Burra Charter and social inclusion', *International Journal of Heritage Studies* 12 (4), 339-55.

Watson, N. (1997) 'Why we argue about virtual community: a case study of the Phish.Net community', in S.G. Jones (ed.) *Virtual Culture: Identity and Communication in Cyberspace*, 102-32. London: SAGE Publications.

Watson, S. (2007) 'Museums and their communities', in S. Watson (ed.) *Museums and their Communities*, 1-23. London: Routledge.

Weiner, A. (1992) *Inalienable Possessions: The Paradox of Keeping-While-Giving*. Berkeley, CA: University of California Press.

—— (1994) 'Cultural difference and the density of objects', *American Ethnologist* 21 (2), 391-403.

Wellman, B. & Gulia, M. (1999) 'Virtual communities as communities', in M.A. Smith & P. Kollock (eds) *Communities in Cyberspace*, 167-94. London: Routledge.

Wertsch, J.V. (2002) *Voices of Collective Remembering*. Cambridge: Cambridge University Press.

Wetherell, M. (2007) 'Introduction: community cohesion and identity dynamics: dilemmas and challenges', in M. Wetherell (ed.) *Identity, Ethnic Diversity and Community Cohesion*, 1-14. London: SAGE Publications.

—— & Potter, E. (1992) *Mapping the Language of Racism: Discourse and the Legitimization of Exploitation*. Hemel Hempstead: Harvester Wheatsheaf.

Whitehead, C. (2005) 'Visiting with suspicion: recent perspectives on art museums', in G. Corsane (ed.) *Heritage, Museums and Galleries: An Introductory Reader*, 89-101. London: Routledge.

Williams, C.C. (2003) 'Developing community involvement: contrast-

Bibliography

ing local and regional participatory cultures in Britain and their implications for policy', *Regional Studies* 37 (5), 531-41.

Willson, M. (1997) 'Community in the abstract: a political and ethical dilemma?', in D. Holmes (ed.) *Virtual Politics: Identity and Community in Cyberspace*, 145-62. London: Routledge.

Witcomb, A. (2003) *Re-Imagining the Museum: Beyond the Mausoleum*. London: Routledge.

Wood, N. (1998) 'The victim's resentments', in B. Cheyette & L. Marcus (eds) *Modernity, Culture and 'The Jew'*. Cambridge: Polity Press.

World Archaeological Congress (1989) *The Vermillion Accord on Human Remains*.

World Stats (2007) 'World Internet Usage', http://internetworldstats.com/stats.htm. Page consulted 14 January 2008.

Wright, P. (1985) *On Living in an Old Country*. London: Verso.

Wylie, A. (2000) 'Questions of evidence, legitimacy and the (dis)union of science', *American Antiquity* 65(2), 227-37.

Young, J. (1989) 'The biography of a memorial icon: Nathan Rapoport's Warsaw Ghetto monument', *Representations* 26 (spring), 69-106.

Yuval-Davis, N. & Silverman, M. (2002) 'Memorializing the holocaust in Britain', *Ethnicities* 2 (1), 107-33.

Zielinski, J. (2007) 'The process of community involvement in community heritage projects', unpublished Masters dissertation, University of York.

Zimmerman, L. (1989) 'Made radical by my own: an archaeologist learns to accept reburial', in R. Layton (ed.) *Conflict in the Archaeology of Living Traditions*, 60-7. London: Unwin Hyman.

——— (1998) 'When data becomes people: archaeological ethics, reburial and the past as public heritage', *International Journal of Cultural Property* 7 (1), 69-88.

——— (2000) 'Regaining our nerve: ethics, values and the transformation of archaeology', in M.J. Lynott & A. Wylie (eds) *Ethics in American Archaeology*, 71-4. Washington: Society for American Archaeology.

——— (2005) 'First, be humble: working with Indigenous peoples and other decendant communities', in C. Smith & H.M. Wobst (eds) *Indigenous Archaeologies: Decolonizing Theory and Practice*, 301-14. London: Routledge.

Zolberg, V.L. (1998) 'Contested remembrance: the Hiroshima exhibit and controversy', *Theory and Society* 27: 565-90.

Index

Aboriginal, 82, 84
aesthetic, 27, 29, 69, 101, 110
African British, 67, 68, 71, 105,
   132-6
Agbetu, Toyin, 67
Alleyne, Brian, 24, 37, 39
Ancient Monuments and
   Archaeological Areas Act
   1979, 27
Anderson, Benedict, 24, 37, 121
Archaeological Heritage
   Management (AHM), 16, 26,
   42, 145; *see also* Cultural
   Heritage Management;
   Cultural Resource
   Management; heritage
   management
Archaeology in Annapolis, 22
archaeology: amateur, 25, 26;
   community-based, 15-17, 95;
   contract, 31; data, 42-3, 53;
   developer-led, 31; expertise,
   26, 33, 42, 53, 84; Indigenous,
   15, 36, 139; postcolonial, 16;
   professional, 22, 25, 26, 28,
   31, 131; public, 15, 16, 21, 25,
   26, 30, 31, 36, 55
architect, 11, 26, 28, 96
architecture, 33, 42, 69, 96
Ashworth, Gregory, 49, 55-8, 60,
   63-4, 65, 135-6

assimilation, 12, 15, 39, 65, 105,
   107, 117
Auschwitz-Birkenau, 46, 47, 56,
   60
Australia, 16, 17, 25, 50, 56,
   82-5, 101, 111, 112
Australian Archaeological
   Association (AAA), 28
authenticity, 27-8, 29, 33, 51, 71,
   84, 97, 123, 125, 128, 136-7
Authorised Heritage Discourse
   (AHD), 33, 34, 43-4, 49, 52,
   53-4, 55, 69, 71, 90, 96, 97,
   100-1; definitions of, 27-31
Ayodhya, 34

Bamyan Buddhas, 34
Bauman, Zygmunt, 11, 24, 142,
   145
Benin Bronzes, 104, 111
bicentenary of the abolition of
   the British slave trade, 66-8,
   71, 109, 114, 115, 135-6, 145
Blair, Tony, 21, 65, 67
Britarch, 126, 130-1
British Archaeological Jobs
   Resource (BAJR), 126
Bulletin Board System (BBS), 126
Byrne, Denis, 28, 33, 45, 50

Cameroon, 13

171

Index